Elite • 204

Sea Peoples of the Bronze Age Mediterranean c.1400 BC–1000 BC

ANDREA SALIMBETI & RAFFAELE D'AMATO

ILLUSTRATED BY GIUSEPPE RAVA

Series editor Martin Windrow

First published in Great Britain in 2015 by Osprey Publishing

PO Box 883, Oxford, OX1 9PL, UK

PO Box 3985, New York, NY 10185–3985, USA

E-mail: info@ospreypublishing.com

Osprey Publishing is part of the Osprey Group

A CIP catalogue record for this book is available from the British Library

Print ISBN: 978 1 4728 0681 9

PDF ebook ISBN: 978 1 4728 0682 6

ePub ebook ISBN: 978 1 4728 0683 3

Editor: Martin Windrow

Index by Fionbar Lyons

Typeset in Sabon and Myriad Pro

Originated by PDQ Media, Bungay, UK

Printed in China through Worldprint Ltd

15 16 17 18 19   10 9 8 7 6 5 4 3 2 1

Osprey Publishing is supporting the Woodland Trust, the UK's leading woodland conservation charity, by funding the dedication of trees.

www.ospreypublishing.com

DEDICATION

To a great woman named Irene

ACKNOWLEDGEMENTS

The authors would like to thank all the scholars and friends who have helped in the realization of this book, as well as the museums and institutions visited.

Firstly, the authors express their deep gratitude to the Library of the Egyptian Museum, Turin, whose staff made available the Epigraphic Survey volumes describing the Medinet Habu temple. Particular acknowledgement is due to Dr David Kaniewsky of the Tel Dweini Project for his help in supplying important iconographic material relating to the invasion of Ugarit by the Sea Peoples.

We would also like to thank the staff of the following: Cyprus Museum, Nicosia; Aghios Mamas Museum, Morphou, Cyprus; British Museum, London; World Museum, Liverpool; IFAO Library, Cairo; and Library of the Deutsches Archäologisches Institut (DAI), Rome and Athens.

The authors are also deeply grateful to Stefanie Groener, BA, for linguistic and editorial assistance; and to Dr Andrei Negin for his illustrations.

Finally, special acknowledgement must be given to our illustrator Giuseppe Rava who, once again, has employed his marvellous talent for the reconstruction of the ancient world.

ARTIST'S NOTE

Readers may care to note that the original paintings from which the colour plates in this book were prepared are available for private sale.
All reproduction copyright whatsoever is retained by the Publishers.
All enquiries should be addressed to:

Giuseppe Rava, via Borgotto 17, 48018 Faenza (RA), Italy

www.g-rava.it

info@g-rava.it

The Publishers regret that they can enter into no correspondence upon this matter.

CONTENTS

SEA PEOPLES OF THE BRONZE AGE MEDITERRANEAN *c.*1400 BC–1000 BC

INTRODUCTION

The term 'Sea Peoples' is given today to various seaborne raiders and invaders from a loose confederation of clans who troubled the Aegean, the Near East and Egypt during the final period of the Bronze Age in the second half of the 2nd millennium BC.

Though the Egyptians presumably knew the homelands of the Sea Peoples, that information has since been lost. Many attempts have been made to determine the origins of the various groups from textual and iconographic evidence, and by study of their material culture as identified in Cyprus and the Levant. This material culture is characterized by locally made Achaean-style pottery, and a considerable but not exclusively Aegean origin has therefore been argued for the multi-ethnic coalition of Sea Peoples.

The reliefs and inscriptions at Medinet Habu in Egypt, together with

A prisoner captured by the Egyptians, possibly a Peleset warrior, wearing a typical 'feathered', reed or leather-strip 'tiara' helmet or headdress. This is a detail from the depiction in the Medinet Habu temple reliefs of Ramesses III's naval victory, *c.*1191–1178 BC. (Author's collection)

Hittite written sources, reveal the emergence of European populations as an influential power in the political and military arena of the Near East and Egypt in the last centuries of the 2nd millennium BC. The movements of 'barbarian' raiders, the crisis of the so-called 'Palatial' system, internal quarrels, and the need for new settlements among the inhabitants of the Aegean area forced defeated leaders to seek refuge and new lands in Western Asia. The records of Pharaoh Ramesses III reveal the repercussions of such Greek migrations and conquests among the Egyptians and neighbouring nations. These newcomers were among the reasons for a sweeping change in Late Bronze Age society, and for the fall of the Palatial societies in Greece as well as the Levant. Scholars have puzzled over whether the Sea Peoples were directly responsible for the collapse of some Late Bronze Age civilizations or were only one of several catalysts, but their movement was certainly one of the most significant migrations in the history of the Mediterranean world.

Many of these 'Northerners' (as they are called in Egyptian texts) were well acquainted with the sea; for at least two centuries the Sherden people had been well known both for their piracy and for their prowess as mercenaries. The shores and islands of the Aegean, as attested by the pottery finds classified as Late Helladic IIIC period (LHIIIC, *c*.1150–1050 BC), were ravaged by confrontations, while many powerful citadels of Late Bronze Age Greece crumbled. Some of these, such as Tiryns in Argolis and Enkomi in Cyprus, became bases for the Sea Peoples and their occasional confederacies. These events may have provoked the Achaean princes to piracy and a search for new lands in the East, confronting the Hittites in Asia Minor who stood in the way of their advances inland from the Aegean. This struggle between the newcomers and the Anatolian population may have been among the causes of the Trojan War.

By about 1200 BC the tide of invasion from Europe had swept across Asia Minor, broken up the Hittite Empire, and spread out over the coasts of Anatolia and the Fertile Crescent; here some of the invaders – also involving Semitic peoples in their migratory movement – began to settle permanently. Amidst all this turmoil, elements of older populations were dislodged; some mixed with the invaders to form new elements of the migratory flow, and others simply fled in search of new homes. As the disintegration of the older states progressed the Sea Peoples increased in numbers and diversity of tribes, extending their attacks towards the south and especially towards the Egyptian empire. The rich cities of the Nile Delta were an attractive prize, and the political situation in Egypt offered an excellent opportunity for new

Heads of various enemies of Egypt, from the Medinet Habu reliefs; three of them represent Aegean warriors with the 'feathered tiara' style of helmet. In Egyptian iconography the artists are careful to differentiate the characteristics of various ethnic groups; the long-haired, bearded figure here may represent a Near Eastern Semitic type, and the man with a fringe and sidelocks a Libyan. (ex Rosellini; author's collection)

settlement. Some of the newcomers allied themselves with the traditional enemies of Egypt, the Libyans, and supported the latters' efforts to settle in the Nile Delta, but this attempt was utterly defeated by the Pharaoh Merneptah in *c*.1207 BC.

However, in Year 5 of the reign of Ramesses III the Egyptian texts record troubles in Syria provoked by the invaders, and in Year 8 a more threatening danger arose. While earlier attacks by the Northerners had been limited to seaborne raids on the coastal regions of the Delta, now the Sea Peoples were moving southward not only in a military invasion but in a comprehensive migration, with their families and possessions, to settle in the Asiatic part of the Egyptian empire. Ramesses III faced invasions by land and sea, as enemy ships seem to have co-operated with the main body moving overland. The pharaoh led out his best forces to meet this threat, including foreign mercenaries, and claims to have won complete victories in the subsequent battles by land and sea.

Groups of defeated Sea Peoples were settled as guardians over the eastern frontiers of Egypt, such as the Philistines who were planted along the Palestinian coast. As the power of the pharaohs slowly diminished into decadence, these settlers created their own kingdoms, taking possession of the Palestinian coastal plain that took its name from them. It has even been suggested that some roamed much further west, since the name of present-day Sardinia resembles that of one of the seagoing groups who were prominent among the Sea Peoples.

CHRONOLOGY (BC)

2000–1700	Egyptian inscription from 'Byblos obelisk' mentions the Lukka.
1430–1385	Annals of Tudhaliya I/II list the Karkisa as taking part in western Anatolian rebellion (Assuwan confederacy) against Hatti.
1386–1321	So-called 'Amarna letters' mention the Sherden, Danuna and Lukka.
1350	Achaean and Sherden mercenaries serve in armies of Pharaohs Akhenaten and Horemheb.
1274	Battle of Kadesh inscriptions of Pharaoh Ramesses II the Great (r.1279–1213) mention the Karkisa and Lukka, together with the pharaoh's Sherden mercenaries.
1260	Treaty of Hittite kings Muwatalli II and Alaksandu of Wilusa binds latter to help former if he campaigns against the Karkisa.
1207	During reign of Pharaoh Merneptah (r.1213–1203), 'Great Karnak Inscription' lists Ekwesh, Teresh, Lukka, Sherden and Shekelesh among 'Northerners' allied with Libyans against Egypt. On the 'Athribis Stele' a list of captured peoples from the Libyan campaign includes Ekwesh of the Sea, Shekelesh, Teresh and Sherden.
Late 13th C:	Letter from king of Ugarit (in Syria) to king of Alashiya (in Cyprus) states that the former is left defenceless against the enemy because all his ships are in 'the land of Lukka'.
Late 13th or early 12th C:	Hittite great king requests from Ugarit extradition of a man who was formerly a prisoner of the Shekelesh (or Tjekker).

1191 or 1178:	Land and sea victories of Pharaoh Ramesses III over confederation of Sea Peoples.
1174–1130	Egyptians plant Peleset in garrisons in southern Canaan, and early 'Philistine' settlements are founded in southern Levantine coastal region.
1114–1064	During 20th Dynasty, under Ramesses XI, Sherden mercenaries are still mentioned in administrative documents as in service of royal house and beneficiaries of lands and goods.

HISTORICAL BACKGROUND & SOURCES

The earliest mention of an ethnic group now considered to be among the Sea Peoples is in Egyptian hieroglyphics on the 'Byblos obelisk'. This mentions *kwkwn* son of *rwqq*, transliterated as Kukunnis, son of Lukka (the Lycian). The next historical evidence is from the 'Amarna letters', representing diplomatic correspondence between 14th-century BC pharaohs and their contemporaries in Canaan, Mesopotamia, Anatolia and the Aegean. At this time the Near East was dominated by a group of 'great kings' with numerous vassal city-states under their influence. It is in the vassal correspondence that the Sea Peoples appear most frequently. The earliest of the letters date from late in the reign of Amenhotep III, and the latest from the reign of Ay (i.e. between *c*.1360 and 1321 BC). The ethnic groups under consideration are the Sherden, Danuna and Lukka.

The Kadesh campaign of Ramesses II, *c*.1274 BC

Some of the Sea Peoples are also mentioned in Pharoah Ramesses II's inscriptions regarding the battle of Kadesh. This battle against the Hittites was one of the most significant events of his reign, and took place in Year 5 of his rule (*c*.1274 BC following the most recent chronology). Although it did not end in a conclusive victory for either side, it did result in a peace treaty between Egypt and Hatti and a period of stability in the ancient Near East. The text is divided into two sections: a bulletin and a poem. In the former, Ramesses mentions, among the confederation of peoples from Canaan and the Mediterranean campaigning alongside the Hittites, the Karkisa and the Lukka. Throughout the text these two peoples are always mentioned in close association with one another. In the poem the composition of the Hittite confederation is again described, but another of the Sea Peoples is mentioned in the context of Ramesses' own soldiers: the Sherden, formerly captured in battle and put to work as mercenary troops. These accounts of the battle are important for what they say about the status of the Sea Peoples at the height of the Egyptian New Kingdom: the Lukka, Karkisa and Sherden were all significant military forces at this time, apparently operating mostly as mercenaries.

The victory of Merneptah, *c*.1207 BC

In the fifth year of the Pharaoh Merneptah (1207 BC) – according to the sources known as the Great Karnak Inscription, Cairo Column, Athribis Stele, and Hymn of Victory (aka the Israel Stele) – King Meryey of the Libyans formed a coalition with several groups of Sea Peoples, and pushed forwards

Sherden mercenaries in the Egyptian army at the battle of Kadesh, c.1274 BC. This image, from one of the Luxor pylons, shows them in simple helmets with neck protection and surmounted by horns and discs, and tunics with extended groin protection. They carry round shields, single spears, and short, curved swords; compare with Plate B1. (ex Rosellini, Plate CVI; author's collection)

into the Nile Delta accompanied by wives, children and belongings (implying that the Northerners intended not only to plunder, but also to settle). Merneptah led an expedition against the invaders, and defeated them after six hours' fighting at the border of the Delta. The Great Karnak Inscription begins with a list of the enemies faced by Egypt: the Labu (Libyans), Ekwesh, Teresh, Lukka, Sherden, and Shekelesh. The Meshwesh (a tribe probably related to the Libyans) appear later in the text. The Ekwesh and Teresh, although traditionally grouped with the rest of the Sea Peoples, do not appear together with the other groups in earlier or later texts.

The most important part of the textual evidence for the purposes of the present study is the list of captives, enemies slain, and plunder. The total number of enemies either killed or brought as living captives to Egypt is 9,376. Most of these were Labu, but the Sea Peoples also account for a large number of the slain: 222 Shekelesh and 742 Teresh are accounted for, though the numbers for the Sherden and Ekwesh have been lost. The list of plunder is interesting for the information that it provides about the material culture of the Sea Peoples and Libyans: 9,111 copper swords were taken from the Meshwesh and Labu, as well as a variety of other weapons, armour, fine vessels, cattle and goats. The Great Karnak Inscription also states that at least three of the Sea Peoples – the Ekwesh, Shekelesh and Sherden – were circumcised, which may offer a clue as to their ethnic origins. (By contrast, it is interesting to note the Old Testament emphasis on the Philistines as an uncircumcised people.)

The historical text on the Cairo Column simply describes the announcement by a messenger to Merneptah of the invasion by the Libyans and their allies: 'Year 5, second month of the third season (tenth month).... The wretched [chief] of Libya has invaded [with]...., being men and women, Shekelesh ...'. The Athribis Stele, similar to the Great Karnak Inscription, consists of an abridged account of the battle (including the Year 5 date), followed by another list of slain enemies, captives and spoils of battle. The numbers generally agree with the other account, with only a few minor differences. The number of dead Sherden is again missing, but the number of Ekwesh killed is given as 2,201.

A
SHERDEN & DANUNA MERCENARIES; EGYPT, 14th CENTURY BC

1: Sherden warrior
The most ancient representation of the 'Shardana' mercenaries in Egyptian art can be found in the reliefs representing the campaigns of Ramesses II in Syria. Note the leather helmet with a single horn; the Aegean/Anatolian style of kilt with a panel pattern and tasselled strings; the shield with multiple bosses; and the long sword of Anatolian origin, copied from one of the specimens published by the archaeologist Flinders Petrie.

2: Danuna warrior
This mercenary wears a typical 'boar's-tusk' helmet of Aegean Greek origin. His bronze spearhead, from the Uluburun shipwreck, has a leaf-shaped blade and a solid-cast seamless socket. This kind of spearhead was probably influenced by weapons made in the northern Balkans and Eastern Europe,

but most examples found in the Aegean are thought to be local products. Note the pectoral amulet and medallion worn by A1 and this figure.

3: Danuna warrior
Copied from the fragmentary Amarna Papyrus, he wears the typical pleated white kilt of Egyptian troops. Here we interpret the headgear alternatively, as a helmet of layered and stitched fabric or leather. His body protection consists of a short-cropped fabric or hide corselet; its upper part is protected by a bronze collar, and there are bronze reinforcements at the other edges. His Aegean Type D sword is copied from the Uluburun specimen. Again, note his ornaments.

4: Egyptian woman
Copied from one of the musicians in the fresco from the tomb of Nebamon; note her double pipes. The domed object worn on the top of her wig is made of a wax that dissolved in warm weather, leaving a perfumed fragrance in the air around her.

Detail from another of the Luxor pylon reliefs, showing the same soldiers cutting off the hands of the slain after the battle of Kadesh. (Author's collection)

The victories of Ramesses III, 1191/1178 *et seq*

The most detailed and best-known texts concerning renewed attacks on Egypt by the Sea Peoples are the inscriptions from the present-day village of Medinet Habu near Thebes in Upper Egypt, where a mortuary temple was constructed for Ramesses III. The interior and exterior wall surfaces are covered with a series of reliefs and texts providing an account of the pharaoh's campaign against the Labu and the 'coalition of the sea' from an Egyptian point of view. The war against the Northerners is described in eight scenes and a long inscription of 38 lines. These refer to Year 8 of Ramesses' reign (1191 BC or 1178 BC, depending on the different dates attributed to his reign, either 1198–1166 or 1186–1155 BC). The campaign is recorded more extensively on the inner north-west panel of the first court.

According to the inscriptions, in that year the Nine Bows (the traditional enemies of Egypt) appear as a 'conspiracy in their isles'. The inscriptions go on to specify the groups involved in the Sea Peoples' confederation: Peleset, Tjekker, Shekelesh, Denyen and Weshesh, who are classified as 'foreign countries'. The hieroglyphics do not mention the Sherden among the invaders, but in two of the Sea Peoples' ships warriors are depicted wearing the horned helmet generally associated with the Sherden. The reliefs are especially significant for their artistic depictions of the Sea Peoples; they provide valuable evidence for the appearance and accoutrements of various groups, and offer clues towards deducing their ethnic backgrounds. To this day, no other source has been discovered that provides such a detailed account of these groups at a specific date in their history.

Other sources

Some Sea Peoples appear in four letters found at Ugarit, Syria, the last three of which seem to foreshadow the destruction of that city in about 1180 BC. The letters therefore date from the early 12th century BC; the last king of Ugarit was Ammurapi or Hammurabi (r.1191–1182 BC), and throughout this correspondence he appears to be quite a young man. In the earliest letter the 'Great King' of the Hittites (presumably Suppiluliuma II) says that he ordered the king of Ugarit to send him the man Ibnadushu for questioning, but that the king was too immature to respond; he therefore wants the prefect to send the man, whom he promises to return. Ibnadushu had been kidnapped by and had resided among a people referred to as 'Shikala' (probably the Shekelesh), 'who lived on ships', and the letter is generally interpreted as showing the Great King's interest in obtaining military intelligence about this people. The last three letters are a set from the Rap'anu Archive by a slightly older King Ammurapi, in which he informed Eshuwara, a senior official of Alashiya, that an enemy fleet of 20 ships had been spotted at sea.

The Anastasi Papyrus is a satirical letter dated to the early Ramessid era (Late Bronze to Early Iron Age); one fragmentary copy can be dated to the reign of Ramesses III, but the name of Ramesses II appears in several passages. The most important section for our purposes deals with the military expedition led by a certain Amenemope, sent to meet a group of foreign enemies at an uncertain location; his assignment is to make provision for the campaign, which he fails to do. These peoples are Sherden, Kehek, Meshwesh, and 'Negroes' (presumably Nubians or Sudanese); this indicates that the Sherden were fighting alongside peoples from North Africa as enemies of Egypt even at this early date, some time within the reign of Ramesses II.

Ramesses III and the Sea Peoples are again mentioned in the Papyrus Harris I, also known as the 'Great Harris Papyrus' – with its 41 metres, the longest papyrus ever found in Egypt. This document, dated to early in the reign of Ramesses IV (r. either 1151–1145 or 1155–1149 BC), was found behind the Medinet Habu temple. It suggests a wider campaign against the Sea Peoples; it does not mention a date, but the event has been connected by scholars with the campaign of Ramesses III's Year 12, as attested by a stele found on the south side of the temple which mentions the Tjekker, Peleset, Denyen, Weshesh and Shekelesh. In the papyrus the persona of Ramesses III says: 'I slew the Denyen *(D'-yn-yw-n)* in their isle and burned the Tjekker and Peleset', thus implying a maritime expedition of his own. He also captured some Sherden and Weshesh 'of the Sea' and settled them in Egypt. As Ramesses III is called the 'Ruler of Nine Bows' in the relief on the east side, these events probably happened subsequent to the battles of his Year 8, when he would have used the victorious fleet for punitive expeditions elsewhere in the Mediterranean.

Decorated gold convex disc from Ashdod, 1100–1000 BC. This fine example of Philistine gold-work, decorated in an Aegean style, has been interpreted by archaeologists as possibly the pommel cap from a sword hilt. An iron spearhead, dated to the reign of Ramesses IV in *c.*1150 BC, has also been found at Ashdod. The Bible attests to the Philistines' military superiority, which was based on their monopoly of iron production in the area. (Ashdod Korin Maman Museum; drawing courtesy Dr Andrei Negin)

11th-century BC terracotta head from Ashkelon, possibly representing a Philistine. (British Museum; author's photo)

The *Onomasticon* of Amenemope or Amenemipit (Amen-em-apt) gives slight credence to the idea that the Ramessid kings settled Sea Peoples in Palestine. Dated to about 1100 BC, it mentions several different groups; after six place names, four of which were in Philistia, the scribe lists the Sherden, the Tjekker and the Peleset, who therefore might be presumed to occupy those cities. The 11th-century BC *Report of Wen-Amon* papyrus also places the Tjekker at Dor, in modern Israel, under the 22nd Dynasty. The Danuna (Denyen) are only mentioned in the *Onomasticon* in the time of Ramesses III. The Lukka are very closely associated with both the Karkisa and the Masa.

IDENTIFICATION OF GROUPS

The Sherden *(S'-r'd-n, S-ar-di-na)*
The Sherden/Shardana were among the first of the Sea Peoples to appear in the historical record; in the Amarna letters (*c*.1350 BC) Sherden are mentioned as part of an Egyptian garrison in Byblos, where they provided their services to the king Rib-Hadda. They appear again during the reign of Ramesses II, in the mid-13th century BC.

PRIMARY SOURCES
Egyptian primary sources mentioning Sea Peoples, by specific group:

Denyen
Amarna letters (El-Amarna tablet 151; Amenophis III/IV)
Medinet Habu (Ramesses III)
Papyrus Harris (Ramesses III)
Onomasticon of Amenemope (late 20th–22nd Dynasties)

Ekwesh
Great Karnak Inscription (Merneptah)
Athribis Stele (Merneptah)

Karkisa
Kadesh inscription (Ramesses II)

Lukka
Obelisk temple hieroglyphics (Byblos obelisk, 2000–1700 BC)
Amarna letters (El-Amarna tablet 38; Akhenaten)
Kadesh inscription (Ramesses II)
Great Karnak Inscription (Merneptah)
Onomasticon of Amenemope (late 20th–22nd D)

Peleset
Medinet Habu (Ramesses III)
Papyrus Harris (Ramesses III)

Rhetorical Stele, Chapel C at Deir el-Medina (Ramesses III)
Onomasticon of Amenemope (late 20th–22nd D)

Shekelesh
Great Karnak Inscription (Merneptah)
Cairo Column (Merneptah)
Athribis Stele (Merneptah)
Medinet Habu (Ramesses III)

Sherden
Amarna letters (El-Amarna tablets 81, 122 & 123; Amenophis III/IV)
Stele of Padjesef (19th–22nd D)
Kadesh inscription (Ramesses II)
Tanis Stele (Ramesses II)
Papyrus Anastasi I (Ramesses II)
Great Karnak Inscription (Merneptah)
Athribis Stele (Merneptah)
Papyrus Anastasi II (Merneptah)
Stele of Stemhebu (late 19th–early 20th D)
Medinet Habu (Ramesses III)
Papyrus Harris (Ramesses III)
Papyrus Amiens (20th D)
Papyrus Wilbour (Ramesses V)
Adoption Papyrus (Ramesses IX)

Papyrus Moscow 169 (Onomasticon Golenischeff; early 21st D)
Papyri British Museum 10326 & 10375 (end 20th D)
Papyrus Turin Museum 2026 (end 20th D)
Onomasticon of Amenemope (late 20th–22nd D)
Donation Stele (Osorkon II)

Teresh
Great Karnak Inscription (Merneptah)
Athribis Stele (Merneptah)
Medinet Habu (Ramesses III)

Rhetorical Stele, Chapel C, Deir el-Medina (Ramesses III)

Tjekker/Sikila (?)
Medinet Habu (Ramesses III)
Papyrus Harris (Ramesses III)
Onomasticon of Amenemope (late 20th–22nd D)
Report of Wen-Amon (22nd D)

Weshesh
Medinet Habu (Ramesses III)
Papyrus Harris (Ramesses III)

Other primary sources mentioning specific groups:

Denyen
Letter to Abi-Milku, king of Tyre, mentions death of king of 'Danuna' (El-Amarna tablet 151)
Hittite sources:
Letters of Ramesses II and Hattusili III
Karatepe inscription (early 1st millennium BC)
Karatepe inscription (8th century BC)

Karkisa
Linear B tablet from Pylos mentions 'Ko-ro-ki-ja' women (An02-292)
Hittite sources:
Annals of Tudhaliya I/II (*Catalogues des textes hittites* 142)
Annals of Mursili II (*Cat. des textes... 61*)
Treaty of Mursili II & Manapa-Tarhunta (*Cat. des textes... 69*)
Treaty of Muwatalli II & Alaksandu of Wilusa (*Cat. des textes... 76*)

Lukka
Letter of king of Alashiya to Akhenaten (El-Amarna tablet 38)
Ugaritic sources:
Letter from king of Ugarit to king of Alashiya (Ras Shamra 20.238)
Hittite sources:
Annals of Tudhaliya I/II (*Cat. des textes... 142*)
Plague prayer of Mursili II (*Cat. des textes... 376*)
Treaty of Muwatalli II & Alaksandu of Wilusa (*Cat. des textes... 76*)
Tawagalawa letter of Hattusili III (*Cat. des textes... 181*)
Annals of Hattusili (*Cat. des textes... 82*)
Suedburg inscription of Suppiluliuma II

Yalburt (Ilgin) inscription – Tudhaliya's military operations
Instruction of Tudhaliya IV to his stewards

Shekelesh
Hittite great king's request to Ugarit (Ras Shamra 34.129)
Tiglath-Pileser III plunders a fortress (Annals text 13)

Sherden
Sherden man defects from Rib-Hadda of Byblos to Abdi-Asirta (El-Amarna 81)
Sherden people under suzerainty of Rib-Hadda of Byblos (El-Amarna 122, 123)

Ugaritic sources:
Lawsuit between two citizens of Ugarit (Ras Shamra 17.112)
Possible use of Sherden as personal name '*Drdn*' (Ras Shamra 19.011)
Contract with unnamed son of a Sherden (Ras Shamra 15.167+163)
Ibshalu receives property of man named '*Mse-er-ta-an-ni*' (Ras Shamra 15.118)
Four Sherden counted (as guards?) in palace (Ras Shamra 15.073)
Five Sherden counted in palace (Ras Shamra 15.015, 15.094, 15.095 & 15.103)
Sherden as recipients in list of wine rations (Ras Shamra 16.165)
Ethnic Sherden name of man '*Al-la-an-se-ri-da-ni*' (Ras Shamra 16.251)

Tjekker/Sikila (?)
Hittite great king's requests from Ugarit (Ras Shamra 34.129)

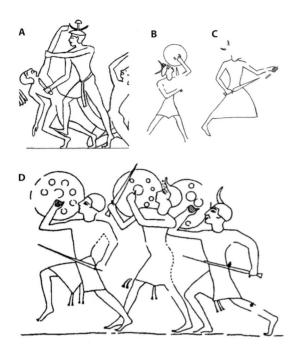

The role that the Sherden played with relation to Egypt varies from one text to another. They appear as a contingent of the Egyptian army in a wide array of sources, including the Kadesh battle inscription of Ramesses II, the Anastasi Papyrus, and the Papyrus Harris of Ramesses III; and as enemies of the Egyptians for the first time under Ramesses II, in the Tanis and Aswan Stelae dated to that pharaoh's Year 2. In later periods they seem to have been mercenaries with no fixed alliances, who might fight either with or against the Egyptians, or both.

At the battle of Kadesh some Sherden were assimilated as the personal guard of Ramesses II. They show up in Egypt again during the reign of Merneptah, now fighting the Egyptians as part of a coalition of Sea Peoples. In the reign of Ramesses III some are probably represented in the Medinet Habu reliefs as fighting alongside the Peleset, but in other scenes they seem to be depicted as mercenaries in the pharaoh's service. While the Medinet Habu inscription does not mention a Sherden presence among the invaders, a chief of the 'Sherden of the Sea' is represented among the prisoners. During the final period of the Bronze Age the Sherden appear in the *Onomasticon* of Amenemope in a list of Sea Peoples occupying the Phoenician coast.

In Egyptian administrative documents subsequent to the reign of Ramesses III (Papyrus Amiens, Papyrus Wilbour, Papyrus of the Adoption, and Papyrus Turin 2026) there is plentiful evidence for settlements, land and goods intended for Sherden mercenaries. This confirms the elite status of such troops in the pharaohs' armies, and in Egyptian society in general. For instance, the Papyrus Amiens states that the king has granted to the Sherden warriors and the royal scribes the agricultural use of land adjacent to the temple of Karnak.

Sherden mercenaries as represented in Egyptian monuments of Ramesses II, *c*.1285 BC. (A) From the Luxor pylons; horns-and-knob helmet, short curved sword or dagger. (B, C & D) from the Ramesseum, Luxor; in D, note plain and single-horn helmets, long swords. (ex Emanuel; drawings by Andrea Salimbeti)

B

SHERDEN MERCENARIES MARCHING TO KADESH, 1274 BC

In the Kadesh inscription of Ramesses II the Great we read of the pharaoh preparing his troops for battle, including the Sherden 'whom he had brought back by victory of his strong arm' (i.e., men captured in a previous campaign and pressed into military service).

1: Regular infantryman

This soldier is copied from the Luxor pylons commemorating the battle of Kadesh. His bronze helmet bowl is similar to many specimens from central Europe, but here it displays horn and disc ornaments, and is worn over the typical Egyptian striped headcloth *(klaft)*. His javelin-head is taken from Anatolian examples; in his left hand he holds a short, single-edged bladed weapon of wavy shape, copied from a specimen found at Tell Es-Sa'idiyeh in modern Jordan.

2: 'Sea Shardana'

This veteran mercenary protects himself, like his countryman of the Royal Guard **(3)**, with a dark buckler, probably of leather, though here lacking bronze bosses; in carvings it is shown to have a single central grip. His bronze stabbing sword (of a class called by some historians a 'rapier', from its function) is 60cm (23.62in) long overall; the colours and decoration of the hilt are copied from the tomb of Ramesses III.

3: Royal guardsman

Copied from the Abu Simbel paintings of the battle of Kadesh. The fluted appearance of the cap-like helmet is interpreted as slices of bone or ivory tusks in an Aegean or Syrian style of construction, and it is surmounted by two horns and a central disc insignia. He is equipped with an Egyptian corselet, apparently provided only to the Royal Guard; it is probably made of quilted linen, and is worn over a stiffened kilt with a triangular frontal piece *(shenti)*. The Medinet Habu reliefs indicate that such armours were fastened at the side by means of loops and bronze buttons. His sword is a rare specimen published by Flinders Petrie, dated to the reign of Ramesses II; it closely resembles those seen in painted sources. The bronze bosses on the bucklers of guardsmen are shown as arranged either in an outer and an inner ring, or an outer ring around a central boss.

Sherden guardsmen of Ramesses II, c.1274 BC, from the temple of Abu Simbel; see Plate B3. (ex Rosellini, Plate CL; author's collection)

The question of their land of origin is still unresolved, since the Egyptian sources only tell us that they came from overseas. Four main hypotheses have been put forward: (1) the region of Sardis in western Anatolia; (2) the Semitic East; (3) the Ionian coast; and (4) the island of Sardinia in the western Mediterranean.

The first is argued by analogy with the fact that ancient authors trace the original homeland of the Tyrsenians to Lydia, so the Sherden are also likely to originate from western Anatolia, where we find the Lydian capital named Sardis, and related names such as Mount Sardena and the Sardanion plain. Accordingly, the Sherden were considered to be on their way from their original home in Lydia to their later home in Sardinia at the time of the upheavals of the Sea Peoples. However, this thesis rests upon nothing more than a perhaps spurious resemblance of names.

Evidence favouring the second hypothesis is the dirk-sword used by the Sherden. This is illustrated in cylinder seals from the East centuries before the first encounter with Egypt, and was among the weapons of the Hittites, thus perhaps indicating a Semitic or Hurrian origin for the Sherden. Furthermore, one Sherden personal name may support this theory: the father of a Sherden on an Ugarit tablet bears a Semitic name, 'Mut-Baal'. It may also be relevant that the image of a captured Sherden chief represented at Medinet Habu closely resembles those of Semites as the Egyptians habitually portrayed them.

According to the third thesis the Sherden might be equated with the Sardonians of the Classical era, a renowned warrior people from the Ionian coast. In the 14th–13th centuries BC the Sherden had already earned a reputation as seaborne raiders.

Sherden mercenary with a typical horned helmet surmounted by a disc, from the early 12th-century BC reliefs at Medinet Habu. Surviving paint-colour shows the helmet as bronze, but the horn is painted light blue, suggesting a contrasting material such as ivory, tin or lead. (ex Epigraphic Survey, Egyptian Museum Library, Turin)

Archaeological evidence presented for the fourth theory draws attention to some similarities of the Egyptian depictions of Sherden with statue-menhirs from southern Corsica; these depict so-called *torre*-builders, who are identical with the *nuraghe*-builders from nearby Sardinia. They give the impression of a society proud of its martial qualities and hence a plausible supplier of mercenaries, in which capacity we encounter the Sherden in the Egyptian and Levantine sources. Furthermore, there are several similarities between Egyptian depictions of Sherden and some of the 11th to 6th-century BC bronze statuettes attested in Sardinia, as well as ship representations and some Bronze Age weapons found in the

island settlements. It is worth mentioning that a 9th/8th-century BC stele from the ancient Sardinian city of Nora bears the word *Srdn* in Phoenician symbols, and seems to be the oldest so far identified in the western Mediterranean.

However, even on the basis of the combined evidence from Corsica and Sardinia, it is difficult to conclude with any confidence if the Sherden originated from or later moved to this part of the Mediterranean. For a start, the Greek sources agree that the original name of the island of Sardinia was in fact Ichnussa; and the description in the Great Karnak Inscription of the Sherden as being circumcised, together with their close resemblance to Semites in Egyptian imagery, makes the second theory more reasonable.

The Peleset *(Pw-r-s-ty)*

These were one of the most significant among the groups that attacked Egypt in Years 5 and 8 of Ramesses III. The name Peleset, which has no earlier occurrence in the Egyptian sources, was identified with the Biblical Philistines by Jean-François Champollion soon after his decipherment of Egyptian hieroglyphics. Nowadays the Philistines are generally considered to have been newcomers in the Levant, settling in their towns of Ashdod, Askelon, Gaza, Ekron, and Gath at the time of the upheavals of the Sea Peoples.

In the Medinet Habu reliefs Ramesses III fights against the Peleset both at sea and on land, and in his battles against the Libyans some warriors who may be identified as Peleset have been recruited (together with Sherden) into the Egyptian army. In the Papyrus Harris, Ramesses III claims to have settled vanquished Sea Peoples, among them the Peleset, in strongholds 'bound in his name'. This has led some scholars to assume that the settlement of the Philistines in Canaan took place under Egyptian supervision. Furthermore,

Many different types of possible Sherden helmets are depicted in the Egyptian reliefs at Luxor c.1280 BC (A, B), Abu Simbel of the same date (C, D) and Medinet Habu, c.1180 BC (all other images). These seem to display horns alone when the Sherden are fighting against the Egyptians; the central disc, presumably in reference to the Egyptian sun god Amon-Re, seems to be added after Sea Peoples are recruited or pressed into the pharaohs' armies. Such depictions show similarity with some Bronze Age/Early Iron Age representations of helmets from the Aegean area, Anatolia, Central/Northern Europe and Italy. (Drawings by Andrea Salimbeti)

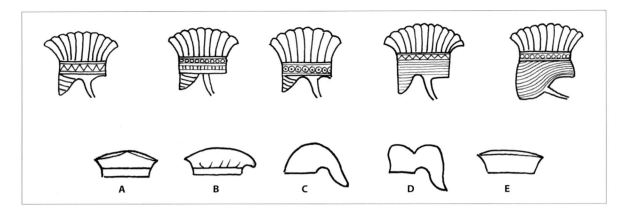

the continuity of Egyptian influence in the hinterland of the Philistine pentapolis might suggest that the Egyptian pharaoh maintained a nominal claim on the land conquered by the Philistines, and considered them as vassals guarding his imperial frontiers. After their settlement in Palestine the Philistines rose to a position of power in the region owing to their military superiority over the local population, as exemplified by the many military engagements described in the Bible.

There are many theories as to the origin of the Peleset-Philistines (Greece, Crete, Illyria, western Anatolia, 'Lands to the East', etc). Based on the various sources, it seemed reasonable to suggest that the Peleset-Philistines did not reach Palestine directly from their original homes but only after a period of wandering Asia Minor and the coasts of the Near East. One theory linked the Peleset to the Homeric Pelasgians, allies of Troy of whom one group lived in Thrace, north-east of Greece. Those Pelasgians would have migrated south, overrunning and fatally damaging Achaean Greek civilization. Shortly afterwards, many would have sailed further south to Crete, where Homer's *Odyssey* mentions Pelasgians. Furthermore, many Biblical passages (Jeremiah 47, Amos 9, Ezekiel 25 & 26) refer to the Philistines' origin as the 'Island of Caphtor'; and in 608 BC they are clearly called Cretans (Sofonia, II, 5). Since many scholars identify Caphtor with Crete, it is widely accepted today that the Peleset were originally Cretan Greeks of the Late Bronze Age. This theory is also supported by the many finds of pottery on Philistine sites that are closely related in ware, shape, paint and decorative concept to examples of the LHIIIC period attested in Greece and the Aegean islands.

A striking piece of evidence from the Near East is the typical 'feather'-topped headdress that recurs on human-shaped coffins discovered in several parts of Palestine. The headdresses moulded on these clay coffins are reminiscent of the Medinet Habu reliefs; minor individual differences in the decoration of the headbands – circles, notches, and zig-zags – might suggest different tribes or clans.

The Tjekker *(T-k-k(r))*
The Tjekker people took part in the campaign against the Egyptians in Year 8 of Ramesses III, and are another major group depicted in the reliefs at Medinet Habu. The Tjekker are also mentioned in the Wen-Amon papyrus of the 11th century BC: the author recalls visiting the city of Dor in modern Israel, which he calls 'a town of the Tjekker', where he was forced to approach its ruler Beder with a complaint about gold stolen from his ships. The Tjekker

warriors fight with short swords, long spears, and round shields. Archaeological evidence from Dor supports Wen-Amon's claim of Tjekker settlement; Stern's excavations discovered a large quantity of Philistine-style bichrome pottery on the site, as well as cow scapulae and bone-handled iron knives similar to those found at Philistine sites. Stern believes this is evidence of a Tjekker (which he calls Sikel) presence at Dor.

Some scholars trace the origins of this group to the Troad, the eastern coastal region of Asia Minor, where they connect the Tjekker with the Teucri people possibly displaced after the Trojan War. Sandars also suggests a connection to the hero Teucer, the traditional founder of a settlement on Cyprus. It is suggested that the Tjekker may have come to Canaan from the Troad by way of Cyprus, and some depictions of warriors found on Cyprus might suggest some connection or shared culture between the Tjekker, Anatolian and Aegean peoples. Some scholars point out that most of the evidence for the origins of the Tjekker people suggests that they came from, or shared a culture with, the people of the Aegean. Redford's conclusions from the reliefs at Medinet Habu also suggest an Aegean connection; he notes that the ships identified as 'Tiakkkr' are more in the Aegean style than any other. The Tjekker warriors are depicted with what he calls 'hoplite-like plumes' on their helmets, often identified as of Greek origin. The archaeological evidence leads to the conclusion that these people were not simply raiders, but a group looking for a place to settle.

Detail from depiction of the triumphal return of Ramesses III from his campaign against Amor, showing prisoners of mixed ethnic types. These appear to be, from left to right: a Libyan, a Shekelesh (see image D opposite), two possible Canaanites or Syrians, and a possible Denyen warrior (see image E opposite).
(ex Epigraphic Survey, Egyptian Museum Library, Turin)

Representation of a warrior killing a gryphon; carved ivory handle, Enkomi, Cyprus, 13th–12th century BC. His torso appears to be protected with inverted-V bands of some kind of 'soft armour'; compare with Plate D3. (British Museum, ex Murray)

The Denyen (D-y-n-yw-n)

Based on New Kingdom Egyptian texts, the Denyen are considered as one of the major groups of the Sea Peoples, and as outstanding seamen and warriors. They are known by many differing names from Egyptian, Hittite, and Classical sources: Danuna, Danunites, Danaoi, Danaus, Danaids, Dene, Danai, and Danaian. The earliest Egyptian text is one of the Amarna letters (mid-14th C BC), relevant to Pharaoh Amenhotep IV's vassal Abi-Milku, the king of the Phoenician city of Tyre. Letter No. 151 mentions the death of a king of 'Danuna'; his brother has succeeded him, and his land is at peace. The Denyen next appear on the temple walls at Medinet Habu during the reign of Ramesses III (early 12th C BC), as part of the Sea Peoples' confederacy attacking Egypt. They are also mentioned in the Papyrus Harris, where Ramesses III himself tells us of his victory. The text of the *Onomasticon* of Amenemope mentions the 'Dene', which Gardiner identifies with the Danuna-Danaoi, perhaps referring to a tribe living on the plain of Argos.

Besides Egyptian texts, Hittite and Classical sources mention the Danuna. The 8th-century BC bilingual inscription from Karatepe tells how King Azitawadda expanded the Plain of Adana and restored his people, the Danunites. In Greek mythology Egypt played an important part in the story of the wanderings of Io and the tragedy of her descendants, the Danais. Various theories as to the homeland of the Denyen have suggested (1) eastern Cilicia, (2) Mycenae, or (3) Canaan.

The first theory is based on the name of Adana, a city in eastern Cilicia, which was known under the name Adaniya by the Hittite king Telepinus (r.1525–1500 BC). According to Barnett, the Denyen lived in Cilicia in the 9th century BC, and caused alarm to the neighbouring Amanus, Kalamu of Sam'al. The 'islands' where Ramesses III situated the Denyen were tiny islets and capes off the Cilician coast. The Denyen are also known from the Karatepe inscription, which mentions the legendary Greek hero Mopsus who is said to have founded Aspendos, which is identified as the town of Azitawadda in Cilicia.

Direct evidence of the settlement of this group is found in the Medinet Habu inscription, where the land called Kode, conquered by the Sea Peoples, is the Egyptian term for Cilicia. Furthermore, a good deal of Achaean-style

THE FIRST EGYPTIAN CAMPAIGN, 1207 BC

Three of these figures represent captives taken by the army of Pharaoh Merneptah, as recorded in the 'Great Karnak Inscription'.

1: Lukka warrior

This prisoner is copied from the Luxor reliefs of Kadesh representing the allies of the Hittites. In their appearances in Egyptian art the Sea Peoples are distinguishable from each other primarily by their headdress. This example, a sort of baggy swept-back turban with a bronze fillet, is also associated with the Teresh and other Hittite allies; it is probably made of linen or felt.

2: Teresh warrior

A common feature of the depicted dress of the Sea Peoples is the kilt with tasselled strings, native to southern Anatolia or the Levant but also widely used by Aegean warriors at that time. The Teresh and the Shekelesh apparently wore banded linen or leather armours. Their headdress was similar to that of the Shasu Bedouins, but also to some low caps of Aegean typology; here it is copied from the Medinet Habu reliefs.

3: Ekwesh warrior

This Achaean warrior from Cyprus is copied from an ivory artefact from Enkomi on that island. He is protected by quilted armour made of leather, felt or other organic material. The decoration of his colourful kilt shows a mixture of Egyptian, Aegean and Levantine styles. Note his helmet, very similar in its structure to those represented in the fragmentary Amarna Papyrus.

4: Egyptian guardsman, *Pdt n šmsw*

This officer carries both a bow and quiver, and a baton or mace as both a symbol of rank and a means of punishment. The *klaft* helmet, with fringed edge, is probably made of leather and padded inside. Note his corselet of quilted and padded linen like that of the Sherden guardsman, Plate B3.

Bronze statuettes from the late 13th-century BC Achaean settlement at Enkomi in Cyprus, representing warriors or deities with horned helmets, as also seen in some Achaean/Aegean art; compare with Plate D1. (Cyprus Museum, Nicosia; author's photo)

pottery of various periods has been found in Cilicia, some of it locally made, and this has been suggested as indicating the arrival of Aegean elements, perhaps as invaders. This event, according to the later Greek sources, is supposed to have happened after the fall of Troy VII in 1180 BC.

A second theory, favoured by many scholars, equates the Denyen with the Danaoi from mainland Acheaen Greece, because all Greeks were referred to as Danaans by Homer. This is a credible suggestion; the Danaans came from Mycenae, and Greek tradition suggests that the Danaoi settled in Argos and were named after the Danaos.

According to the third theory the Denyen originated in Canaan. By this hypothesis the Denyen and other Sea Peoples returned to the Levant as a counter-migration, while other Denyen went to the Aegean and Mycenae and became known as Danaans. The Denyen were a major part of the confederation in the Levant that attacked Egypt with the other Sea Peoples, especially the Peleset, and participated in the sea battle against Ramesses III. Others went to Asia Minor, and some of the Sea Peoples returned to the Levant, where these Denyen were accepted into the confederation of the tribes of Israel called Dan.

The Biblical data shows that at a certain stage of its settlement the Tribe of Dan was very close to the People of the Sea. From the historical and mythological sources, it is possible to construct the following theory. The tribe of the Danai originated in the East, and the introduction of the alphabet to Greece is attributed to it. Its members were outstanding seamen who had a special connection with sun worship. The association with the Tribe of Dan is because they formed two different tribes (the Danites and the Danai) with identical names and similar characteristics, who operated in the same geographical region and period, or had a strong link between them, and possibly a certain measure of identity.

The Shekelesh (*S'-r'-rw-s'*)

This is one of the most obscure groups, but it is clear that they played an important role in the military conquests of the Sea Peoples' coalition. They are only mentioned in passing in the ancient texts, such as the annals of Ramesses III from Medinet Habu and the Ugaritic texts. The group is also mentioned in the Kom el-Ahmar Stele from the reign of Merneptah.

The Shekelesh officially make an appearance attacking Egypt in around 1220 BC, and again, invading the Delta, in 1186–1184 BC. One of the earliest mentions of them occurs early in the reign of the Pharaoh Merneptah. When he confronted the Libyan invasion he faced not just one hostile tribe, but an alliance of Sea Peoples groups: the Meshwesh, the people of the island of Kos, and the Lycians, who were the major forces and urged smaller tribes like the Sherden, Tyrsenoi, and Shekelesh to assist in the fight against the Egyptians. When the two armies met the Egyptians, although suffering major losses, eventually slaughtered over 9,000 of the Sea Peoples' coalition, and Merneptah records that he killed 222 Shekelesh warriors. Years later, Ramesses III would finish the job that Merneptah began and (or so he claims) completely wipe out the Sea Peoples.

The reliefs and inscriptions at Medinet Habu only mention the Shekelesh briefly, but we are able to get a glimpse of what a Shekelesh soldier might have looked like. Among the other groups the Shekelesh (and the Teresh) stand out as wearing cloth headdresses and a medallion on their breasts, and carry two spears and a round shield. However, because the inscription related to the sea battle only mentions the Peleset, the Weshesh (normally associated with the 'feathered' headdress), and the Shekelesh, some scholars suggest that the warriors with horned helmets, normally identified with the Sherden, could instead have been the Shekelesh. They also suggest that the Sherden are probably the men represented with horned helmets incorporating a central disk or knob.

The Shekelesh's place of origin has been considered to be Sagalassos in Pisidia. Some scholars, such as N.K. Sandars, believe that the Shekelesh came from south-eastern Sicily. Other sources tell us that the 'Sikeloy' were not the original inhabitants of Sicily, but migrated there from peninsular Italy. In the 8th century BC Greek colonists on Sicily came across a group of people known as the Sikels, who they believed had come from Italy after the Trojan War.

The Ekwesh *('-k-w'-s')*
Scholars generally accept that the name Ekwesh or Akwash is the Egyptian equivalent of Achaean and Ahhiyawa in Hittite texts, so forming another group of Bronze Age Greeks among the Sea Peoples. According to the best reading of the numbers inscribed at Karnak, there were 1,213 Ekwesh casualties in Merneptah's 1207 BC campaign; they were the largest group among the Sea Peoples, and formed the core of this force. Further, the Karnak inscriptions clearly imply that the Akwash/Ekwesh were circumcised. Hardly anyone thinks that the Greeks of the Bronze Age were circumcised, but of course, no one really knows. It is certainly possible that the Ekwesh were Achaeans, but which Achaeans? Not only were there Achaeans on the mainland and Crete but also in Cyprus, on the Anatolian coast and on the island of Rhodes.

As far as Cyprus is concerned, it is possible that at the time when the major Achaean centres in the Peloponnese were destroyed or abandoned, the fortified settlements at Maa-Palaeokastro, Hala Sultan Tekke near Larnaca,

Scale from a bronze armour bearing the mark of Ramesses II, 13th century BC. Important recent discoveries excavated together at Kanakia, on the south-west tip of the island of Salamina (Salamis), included tools, Cypriot pottery, and this scale from a bronze body armour. This is possible evidence that Salamina warriors had fought as mercenaries in the army of Ramesses II. (Drawing by Dr Andrei Negin, Salamina Archaeological Museum)

Representation of Achaean aristocratic archer and hunting party, Cyprus, 13th–12th century BC. Note the chariot with six-spoke wheels, and the headdress and kilt of the axeman at the far right. The central figure in this detail from an ivory gaming box from Tomb 58 at Enkomi is the clearest representation of scale armour from an area where the presence of the Sea Peoples is attested. Compare with Plate D2; the style of the figure shows both Aegean and Near Eastern influences. (British Museum, ex Murray; author's photo)

and especially Enkomi were constructed or re-colonized by people from both the Greek mainland and Crete (Peleset?), who may also have brought Anatolians with them. Refugees may have settled near major urban centres in Cyprus (with which they or their forefathers were already familiar from earlier trade connections), and gradually expanded into these centres. The new wave of immigrants brought with them the so-called 'Mycenaean IIIC1' pottery style, which is found at all the major Late Bronze Age centres in Cyprus (Enkomi, Kition, Palaeopaphos, etc). The same pottery is also found in the first settlements of the Peleset in the Levant and in the Fertile Crescent. These Achaeans, together with other groups of Achaeans from Anatolia and nearby islands, were probably the Ekwesh of the Egyptian sources. This interpretation is strengthened by the very similar material culture shown in Late Bronze Age Cyprus and the representations of the Sea Peoples group in the Egyptian sources.

In their settlements on the Anatolian coast the Achaeans were neighbours of the Lukka, and might have allied with that group in various ventures. Legends preserved by the Greeks remember close contacts with the Lukka or Lycians. It is thus believable that Achaeans from the Anatolian coast could have been caught up with their Lukka neighbours in events, whatever they may have been, that impelled them to sail for the coast of Libya or Egypt. A possible reference that the Achaeans were among Egypt's attackers is from the *Odyssey* (Book XIV):

I had been home no more than a month, enjoying my family and wealthy estate, when the spirit urged me to fit out some ships and set sail for Egypt, along with my godlike comrades. Nine ships in all were readied, and quickly the great crew gathered, for six days… On the fifth day we came to the great Egyptian river, and there in that fair-flowing stream we moored our ships. Then I told my trusty companions to stay by the ships and guard them, and I sent some scouts to high vantage points to get the lay of the land. But the crews gave way to wanton violence, and, carried away by their strength, they began to pillage and plunder the fine Egyptian farms. They abducted the women and children and murdered the men. But their cries were heard in the city, and at dawn the whole plain was full of foot-soldiers and chariots

D SEA BATTLE OFF ALASHIYA, CYPRUS, c.1200–1190 BC

The Hittite 'great king' Suppiluliuma II wrote that he attacked ships from Alashiya at sea and burned them, subsequently landing on the shore of Alashiya and bringing the enemy to battle. Several finds in the city of Enkomi and other areas of Cyprus reveal the presence there of Sea Peoples.

1: Alashiyan priest-king
This Achaean king is reconstructed from the famous statuette found in Enkomi representing a horned warrior-deity. Note his sceptre with two sitting eagles on the spherical head, and his rich gold jewellery and ornaments, all from Enkomi.

2: Cypriot aristocratic *eqeta*
This elite warrior is copied from an ivory gaming box found at Enkomi, with decoration representing a hunting scene. His scale armour is reconstructed from fragments recovered in Cyprus. His helmet is from the 'Enkomi seal'; it shows elements of Aegean and Syrian features, such as the embossed bowl divided into strips, and the horns mounted at the sides of the brow.

3: Ekwesh warrior
Two ivory carvings from Enkomi, representing fighting scenes against a lion and a gryphon, show warriors protected by corselets made with inverted-V bands of some organic material. Similar 'soft armour' is also apparently worn by many of the Sea Peoples warriors represented in the Medinet Habu reliefs.

4: Alashiyan Ekwesh warrior
This foot-soldier, copied from the same ivory box as D2, is armed with both a dagger and a battle-axe. He wears the kilt, *kiton* and 'feathered' headgear typical of depictions of the Sea Peoples. The headdress in this Cypriot context confirms the Aegean origins of similar warriors represented in the Medinet Habu reliefs.

The 'Enkomi Seal' from Cyprus, dated to the late 13th century BC. It clearly represents a bearded warrior wearing an embossed helmet with side-horns; compare with Plate D2. (Cyprus Museum, Nicosia; author's photo)

and the flashing of bronze... Thus, with keen bronze, their men cut us down by the dozen, and they led up others to their city as slaves...

Of course, it cannot be known if this passage preserves a memory of the invasion of Egypt during the reign of Merneptah, or of other raids on Egypt by Greeks of the Late Bronze Age.

The Teresh *(Tw-ry-s')*

The Teresh or Tursha are mentioned during Year 5 of Merneptah's reign (*c.*1207 BC), in the Great Karnak Inscription, as being among the enemy coalition faced by Egypt. During the reign of Ramesses III a Teresh chief is shown together with other captive Sea Peoples in the Medinet Habu reliefs. Furthermore, in Tomb 23 from Gurob the archaeologist W. Flinders Petrie found the mummy of An-en-Tursha, a Teresh butler at the court of Ramesses III. This well-preserved mummy still shows fair hair, confirming that he was not native to Egypt or Africa.

Several possibilities exist which may identify the Teresh as Anatolians. First to be considered are the Trojans: Troy appears in a Hittite record as 'Taruisa', and it is a reasonable assumption that the people of Taruisa called themselves by some name close to this. The period of the attack of the Sea Peoples' coalition is compatible with some of the military events that occurred in the area of Troy. It is to be expected that there were many Trojan refugees, among whom some would attempt to survive by their wits and their swords.

A second possibility might be the Tyrsenians, a group of pirates with 'well decked ships' mentioned in two works of about 700 BC, and in a poem known as *Hymn to Dionysus* which tradition attributes to Homer. During the Classical period Herodotus and Thucydides mention them under the name Tyrrhenians. Herodotus places these people in Lydia, and Thucydides remarks that they were known to live on the island of Lesbos, offshore from Lydia. Lydia is the Classical-period name for the land which in the Bronze Age was Arzawa, and possibly part of the Seha River Land, an area located not far south of Taruisa. Some scholars suggest that the Tyrsenians may be related to the Etruscans: in fact the Tyrrhenian Sea – the name is derived from a Greek term – still survives as a name for the waters between western Italy, Corsica and Sardinia.

A third theory shifts the geographic focus to the south-east coast of Anatolia. In a Hittite record containing a list of cities the names Kummanni, Zunnahara, Adaniya and Tarsa appear together. The last two are most likely the cities of Adana and Tarsus, and it is certain that Tarsus was in existence in the Bronze Age. If the Egyptians were to ask a man of Tarsus where he came from, he might point in a northerly direction and answer 'from Tarsa', 'Tarsha' or 'Tarssas', and this would be written down by Egyptians as *T-r-s* or *T-r-sh*. Tarsus is close to the coast, and in later times was an important port; furthermore it is not a great distance from the coast of Lycia/Lukka, and there was probably frequent contact between these peoples.

The Karkisa

The Karkisa appear to be one of the minor tribes; most of the ancient references are only passing mentions, and in many cases it is unclear whether they are referring to a group of people or a geographical region.

The first mentions of Karkisa occur during the reigns of Ramesses II of Egypt and Muwatalli of the Hittite Empire. In the former case, in both the bulletin and the poem referring to the battle of Kadesh the Karkisa are mentioned in lists of tribes that had joined forces with the Hittites, without further details. The Hittite record reinforces the idea of this alliance; the annals mention that Muwatalli sent a person to the people of Karkisa, whom he paid to protect this man from his own brothers. The man then sided with an enemy of Muwatalli, but when captured he begged to become once again a vassal of the great Hittite king. In this story the Karkisa are represented as allies of the Hittites, which fits their description by Ramesses II. They make one final appearance in ancient literature, being mentioned in the *Onomasticon* of Amenemope in a exclusively geographical reference to the land of Lukka. Some scholars place the Karkisa in south-west Asia Minor; Barnett mentions specifically that the Karkisa are associated with the Hittite area of Caria, which is on the south-western tip of Anatolia.

The Lukka *(Rw-kw)*

The Lukka were mentioned in some ancient texts, but rarely in any source more detailed than simple lists. There is no clear evidence of where exactly the Lukka (Lycian) lands were, but scholars have proposed some possibilities.

One theory is that the Lukka were scattered in western Anatolia, Caria being one of several areas where they were found. Over time they broke down the rule of the Hittites by persistent raiding. In the Ugarit tablets we find letters from the Ugarit king to the king of Alashiya, stating that the former will send a fleet to the coast of Lukka to defend the passage from the Aegean to the Mediterranean; Lukka territory reached the 'coast', but it is unclear if he means the Aegean or the Mediterranean coast. These Lukka

This fragment of a painted papyrus from Tel el-Amarna, Egypt, dated to the 14th-century BC reigns of Akhenaten or Horemheb, shows a group of warriors wearing a short-cropped corselet and a helmet of possible Greek type. Outlined in red and coloured in yellow with vertical demarcations, this might represent the 'boar's-tusk' type, or simply a quilted fabric design as used by Cypriot Achaean warriors as late as 1100 BC. In any case, the un-Egyptian features argue the representation of mercenaries from the Aegean world. The short-cropped corselet on the main figure strengthens the suggestion that these warriors came from the Achaean colonies on Cyprus, in a period of well-developed commercial relations between Egypt and the Aegean. (ex Schofield & Parkinson; courtesy DAI Library, Rome)

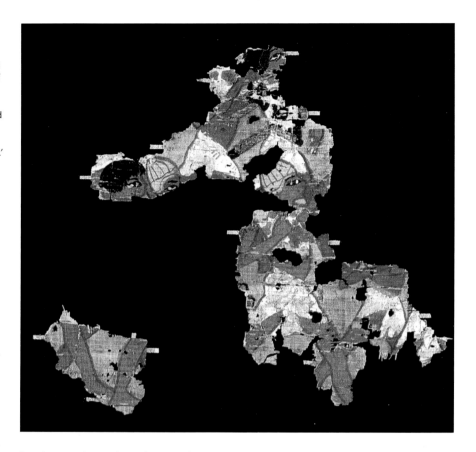

lands are also referred to as the Xanthos Valley. The Lycians had a series of kingdoms, called Arzawa lands, under Hittite suzerainty; these seem to have had no real political power, since there is no evidence of treaties with the Hittites or of any named Lukka king.

According to Hittite texts the Lukka were a rebellious people, sea-goers, and easily swayed by foreign influences. During the mid-15th century BC, early in the Egyptian New Kingdom, Lukka was part of an alliance against the Hittites with 22 other countries, called the Assuwan confederacy, but this was defeated by the Hittite king Tudhaliya I. From Pritchard, we have a translation of a Hittite prayer in which the Lukka are referred to as denouncing the Hittite sun goddess Arinna. In this same prayer the Lukka are said to be attacking and destroying the Hatti land, along with other peoples. These examples tell us that the Lukka were in the area, were belligerent, and had some measure of power. They made yearly attacks by sea on the king of Alashiya's lands, and so were considered as pirates. The Amarna letters include an appeal for aid from the Alashiyan king to the Pharaoh Akhenaten, and reassurance that the former was not siding with these Lukka people.

From the time of Ramesses II, the poem from the battle of Kadesh mentions the Lukka as being an ally of the defeated prince of Kheta. The Great Karnak Inscription of Merneptah, related to his victory over the invading Libyans and their northern seaborne allies, gives a supposed number of 200 casualties inflicted on the Lukka (which is insignificant in comparison to the 6,539 Libyans claimed as killed). Barnett notes that though there are many depictions of Sea Peoples, none exist of the Lukka.

The Weshesh *(W-s-s)*

The Weshesh were part of the combined force of Sea Peoples that attacked Egypt during the reign of Ramesses III. Little is known about them, though once again there is a tenuous link to Troy. The Greeks sometimes referred to the city of Troy as Ilios, but this may have evolved from the Hittite name for the region, Wilusa, via the intermediate form Wilios. If the people called Weshesh by the Egyptians were indeed the Wilusans, as has been speculated, then they may have included some genuine Trojans. Some scholars associate the Weshesh with Iasos, Assos or Issos in Asia Minor, or with Karkisa (Caria).

The 'Lost Tribes of Israel' have proved irresistibly attractive to many scholars, and some have even theorized that the Weshesh, like the Denyen, became part of the Israelite confederacy, in this case as the Tribe of Asher, the eighth son of Jacob, who settled in Egypt. The tribe may be the same as the Weshesh mentioned in Egyptian accounts (the 'W' of Weshesh is a modern invention for ease of pronunciation, and Egyptian records refer to the group as the Uashesh). By this hypothesis, the Weshesh were thus the Semitic part of a tribal confederation that also included Peleset (Philistines), Danua (possibly Tribe of Dan), Tjekker (thought to mean 'of Acco', and thus possibly referring to Manessah), and Shekelesh (thought to mean 'men of Sheker', and thus perhaps referring to Issachar).

Mercenary service: a summary of the evidence

Possible early evidence of Aegean mercenaries within the Egyptian army is a fragment of papyrus found in December 1936 by John Pendlebury, in HR43.2 on the eastern edge of the Central City at El-Amarna, in association with diverse items including a complete Achaean vase. The fragment appears to be from a purely pictorial papyrus depicting a battle between Egyptians and Libyan warriors. Coming to the aid of the Egyptians are a number of warriors who, while wearing typical Egyptian white kilts, are equipped with helmets, and various types of what may plausibly be argued to represent fabric or leather armour. Neither the helmets nor the two identifiable types of armour are present elsewhere in the Egyptian iconographic record, and they thus seem to identify a people other than those usually depicted in Egyptian paintings.

It has been forcefully argued that the headgear depicted on the papyrus

Detail of a hunting party at the court of Ramesses III, from Medinet Habu, early 12th century BC. These Sea Peoples mercenaries are mainly Sherden, but the two at the right might be Shekelesh; they are distinguished by their different types of headgear, Anatolian-style kilts, and short, wavy-bladed Canaanite swords. (ex Epigraphic Survey, Egyptian Museum Library, Turin)

should be identified as boar's-tusk helmets. Made principally of leather but covered with pieces of sliced boar tusks, these are strongly associated with Achaean elite warriors between 1600 and 1250 BC. This identification is strengthened by the find of a piece of boar's tusk, with perforations for attaching it to a leather base, during excavations at Qantir, the site of the Ramessid capital Pi-Ramesse in the eastern Delta. The body protection worn by the warriors has close parallels with known Aegean types of corselets. Consequently, the warriors depicted on the papyrus most probably represent Achaean Greeks, apparently in the service of the pharaoh. This interpretation is supported by the recent discovery at Kanakia, on the island of Salamina (Salamis), of a bronze scale from a corselet bearing the stamp of Pharaoh Ramesses II.

These finds would seem to offer evidence that Achaean mercenaries were serving in the Egyptian army at different periods. During the 19th Dynasty the Egyptians made extensive (and risky) use of non-native troops to make up for a decline in military enthusiasm under the previous dynasty. As we have seen, one group who served in this capacity were the Sherden, who had been in mercenary service since at least the reign of Akhenaten (Amarna letters). The first evidence for the submission of captured Sherden to Ramesses II is found in the Stele of Tanis; the Kadesh inscription mentions them in regular service, and they appear at the siege of the Syrian cities of Tunip and Dapur. In the Papyrus Anastasi, where the presence of foreign troops in the Egyptian army is attested, the Sherden are part of a group of 'specialists of war' which also includes Libyans, Nubians and Kehek. The Medinet Habu inscriptions mention them as mercenaries under Ramesses III, when they were involved in the land battle against the other Sea Peoples and in the bloody war against the Labu (Libyans). A more complex situation is described in the Papyrus Harris I (reign of Ramesses IV), where Sherden are mentioned both among the Egyptian auxiliary troops and among the prisoners of war forcibly recruited by the pharaoh and settled in garrisons scattered throughout his empire.

The social importance of Sherden mercenaries in the Egyptian world is recorded, apart from the already-quoted Papyrus Amiens, in a second important document, the Papyrus Wilbour. Here 42 Sherden are mentioned as beneficiaries of land grants of the same type as given to officials and priests. This was an important professional benefit, ensuring all rights of ownership including, for instance, the employment of farmers and servants. This document also suggests equal treatment between the Sherden and their Egyptian officers, the 'standard bearers'. Unlike other groups of mercenaries these warriors are not led by an Egyptian regular officer but are organized into companies specifically commanded by a 'standard bearer of the Sherden', i.e. by an officer from among their number.

The successful social integration of Sherden mercenaries at the end of the 20th Dynasty (reign of Ramesses XI) is highlighted in other documents, including the Papyrus of the Adoption, the *Onomasticon* Golenisheff, the Papyrus of Turin 2026 and the Papyri British Museum 10326 and 10375. The last relevant document is the Stele of Donation from Helwan, dating from Year 16 of the reign of Osorkon I in the 9th century BC, which mentions a donation of lands including 'the Sherdens' fields'.

Outside Egypt, the presence of Sherden mercenaries is first attested in the Amarna letters, where Rib-Hadda of Byblos says that he has killed rebels, and makes reference to the presence (perhaps within his garrison) of *am [êlu] si-ir'-da-nu*. A second group of documents mentioning Sherden mercenaries are the Ugaritic texts dating from the 14th to 12th centuries BC; here the

Sherden are beneficiaries of land grants, and serve as *mdrglm* and *tnnm*, 'fighters'. A final reference to the presence of Sherden in Ugarit is in letter KTU 2.61 (2114) addressed to the *drdn* of the city and mentioning dangerous incursions by marauders (Sea Peoples?) against an Ugaritic city. The context of this purely military message has convinced some scholars that the Sarridanu (*drdn*) could have been the commander of the Ugarit garrison, perhaps residing in the 'Minor Palace' of the city.

Piracy

Piracy or raids against Egypt were not unusual between the 14th and 12th centuries BC. As early as the 14th century BC one of the Amarna letters has the king of Egypt probably accusing people from Alashiya of participating in raids against Egypt. The 13th-century BC Tanis Stele of Ramesses II describes the Sherden as pirates who conduct raids from ships. A 12th-century BC Ugarit document shows that seaborne raids seem to have been on a larger scale, probably employing as many as 20 ships, with the number of men between 400 and 1,000. Sailing time would have been relatively short: probably five to seven days at sea from the Dodecanese, south-western Anatolia or the southern Levant, and 10–13 days returning. If the raiders established a forward base camp in the islands of the Delta (perhaps 'the islands in the middle of the Great Green'), the duration of the entire expedition could have reduced to at most 20 days – short enough to have been worth the risk of leaving home.

These symbolic representations of leaders of the Sea Peoples captured in the 'War of the Eighth Year', from Medinet Habu, are one of the few Egyptian sources that give clear identification of the different groups in both imagery and script: (A) Sherden of the Sea; (B) Tjekker; (C) Teresh of the Sea; and (D) Peleset. (Author's collection)

CLOTHING & EQUIPMENT

Clothing

The implication of the Egyptian inscriptions at Medinet Habu is that all the confederated peoples – Peleset, Tjekker, Shekelesh, Denyen and Weshesh – were represented at the land battle, but in appearance the warriors depicted in the reliefs are (except for some specific details) noticeably homogeneous; for instance, all wear the 'feathered tiara' headdress, and none the distinctive horned helmet. Since the Egyptians were normally fairly careful in recording such details, we may infer that this representation is close to reality, and thus that the coalition of Sea People warriors present on this occasion displayed common costume and weaponry and perhaps shared a similar material culture.

Mostly the Sea People are represented with simple tunics, below which hangs an Aegean/Anatolian-style kilt. This sometimes terminates in strings decorated

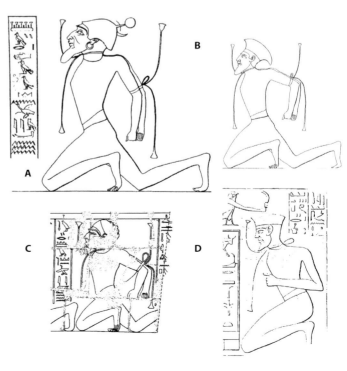

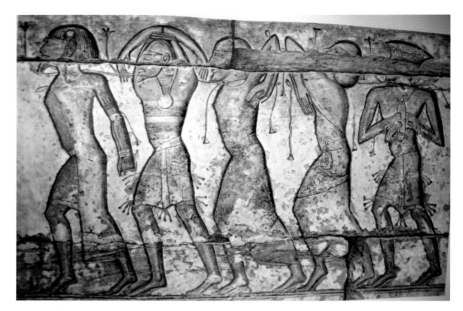

A well-preserved painted relief at Medinet Habu showing leaders taken captive by Ramesses III in his Asiatic and Libyan campaigns; note the different methods of tying their arms. Second left, following a Libyan or Canaanite, is a Teresh or Shekelesh leader (see Plate C2), and the manacled prisoner at far right seems to have the Peleset or Tjekker headdress. The enlarged detail of the Teresh/Shekelesh figure (below left) shows a medallion; the coloured pattern and tasselled strings of an Aegean/Anatolian-style kilt; and bands of 'soft armour' protecting his lower torso. The tasselled strings are identically illustrated (below right) on the Peleset/Tjekker figure.(ex Epigraphic Survey, Egyptian Museum Library, Turin)

with tassels, as often found in Aegean contexts (as in the warrior graves at Kos, variously dated between 1300 and 1200 BC). These tasselled strings are often disposed in five groups of three, at the sides and centre of the kilt. Some kilts, divided into two or more vertical and horizontal rows of coloured panels, perhaps indicate distinctive groups. The Sherden serving Ramesses II as mercenaries or bodyguards are represented with typical Egyptian infantry outfits of a long kilt and sometimes a quilted corselet, while all except one of those serving Ramesses III at the storm of Tunip wear the Aegean/Anatolian kilt. Some well-preserved Egyptian reliefs show the Sea Peoples' clothing as very colourful, in various designs and shades of red, white, blue and green – again, very similar to contemporary Aegean patterns – and alternating panels of red and blue are divided by white bands. Sometimes the kilt is the only garment worn by warriors who seem be bare-chested, but the present state of the reliefs does not allow an accurate identification of possible upper garments. The feet are bare or shod with short sandals.

Sometimes beards of Aegean type are visible, as for instance in the pointed beards of the Tjekker prisoners presented to the god Amon-Re by Ramesses III in a relief at Medinet Habu.

Defensive equipment:
Helmets

The Medinet Habu reliefs are fundamental to any reconstruction of the war gear of the Sea Peoples. The battle scenes provide a wealth of information about the appearance of the various groups, and provide hints as to their ethnic backgrounds.

Both Sherden and (perhaps) Shekelesh wear horned helmets, but the Sherden (always?) also incorporate a knob or disc. The

Rhyton of faience from Enkomi, late 13th century BC, representing a warrior with a dagger (right). Both figures wear a high conical helmet with a flowing crest attached to the upper knob. (Cyprus Museum, Nicosia; author's photo)

'Egyptian mercenary' Sherden typically wear helmets topped with horns and a disc, and are equipped with spears, swords, and round embossed shields. The Sea Peoples named at the famous battle of the Delta are the Peleset, Shekelesh, and Weshesh of the Sea; the contingents shown on the monuments are probably of these peoples, even if warriors wearing horned helmets are clearly depicted. Such helmets were probably worn by other Sea Peoples apart from the Sherden, as attested by the wide range of horned helmets represented in LHIIIC Anatolian and Aegean figurative art.

The simultaneous presence of 'free' Sherden among the invaders is confirmed by the representation at Medinet Habu of a captive called 'Sherden of the Sea', probably to distinguish this group from the Egyptian-employed mercenaries – yet he too wears a horned helmet with a central disc. A similar prisoner, wearing the same helmet, is brought before the god Amon-Re among other captive leaders. Most relevant archaeological evidence for horned helmets comes from Cyprus, where, at Enkomi, a settlement of Achaean Sea People flourished in about 1200 BC.

Also at Enkomi, some military headgear represented on ivory items seems to recall the helmet worn by the Achaean mercenaries pictured in the above-mentioned fragmentary papyrus from Tel el-Amarna, attesting its use from *c.*1350 until at least the end of the Bronze Age. (An alternative interpretation of the striped appearance of the bowl of this helmet would suggest not slices of boar's tusk but a simpler construction of leather or felt, as in Plate A3.)

The 'feathered' or 'reed' headgear is associated with the Peleset, Tjekker, Denyen and Weshesh. Many warriors on the Medinet Habu reliefs wear this typical Aegean/Anatolian headdress, also visible on more-or-less contemporary representations from Cyprus, Crete, Malta and Sardinia. It was formed on a bronze headband embossed with studs, rings, triangles or vertical bars (according to Yadin, possible distinctions of different groups or ranks). From this, a level-topped array of

Head of a warrior from Crete, 13th–12th century BC. This interesting head carved from stag's-horn shows a bearded man who seems to wear a 'feathered' headdress, recalling the headgear of the Sea People as represented in Egyptian and Cypriot art. His general aspect shows a striking resemblance to the warrior represented on the Enkomi Seal, and to the so called 'Agamemnon mask' from Mycenae. (British Museum; drawing by Dr Andrei Negin)

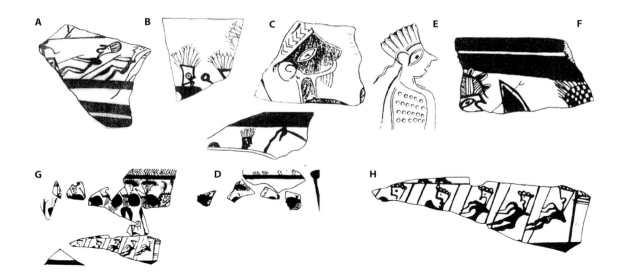

Fragments of pottery with depictions of Aegean warriors with possible 'feathered tiara' headgear: (A, B, D & F) from Serayia in the island of Kos; (C) from Mycenae; (E) from Ugarit, Syria; (G & H) from Bademgedigi Tepe, western Anatolia. (Drawings by Andrea Salimbeti)

'floppy strips' of leather, reeds, straw, horsehair, or perhaps sometimes feathers, protrudes upwards. Traces of light blue paint are visible on this part of a man's headdress from Medinet Habu. Metal headbands for such 'feathered headgear' are attested in several contemporary images from Aegean areas as well as the south, east and central Mediterranean. For example, the still undeciphered Phaistos disk dated to *c.*1700 BC shows the head of a man crowned with possible feathers very similar to the headgear of the Peleset depicted at Medinet Habu; beside him is a possibly embossed shield like some of those shown in the Egyptian reliefs. These elements may also support the theory that the Peleset were originally Cretans.

This 'tiara-like' helmet was sometime equipped with neck protection, and was secured with a chinstrap fastened by two small strings. Important finds of bronze elements for such helmets have been made in warrior graves dated

THE FALL OF THE HITTITE EMPIRE, *c.*1200–1180 BC

1: Lukka prince
The lavish equipment of this Sea Peoples leader is strongly Aegean in fashion, especially his plate bronze armour. Note his long, heavy ash spear, as described in Homer's *Iliad* for the Lukka leader Sarpedons. The description of his shield (*Iliad*, XII, 295) recalls the kind of shield visible in the Egyptian iconography: 'Holding his round shield before him, bronze hammered by the smith and lined with ox-hides stitched with gold around the rim...'

2: Weshesh warrior
Note again the 'tiara' helmet in bronze with leather (?) 'plumes'. The headband is in two rows, the upper decorated with a line of bosses and the lower with dots and pieces of coloured glass; the chinstrap is well detailed in the Egyptian sources. The bronze 'lobster-type' cuirass is formed with an upper breast protector, and below this bands of inverted-V shape over the torso. The rounded, embossed shoulder-guards support two protective strips for the upper arms, as

in the specimens from Thebes. Below the cuirass he wears a knee-length kilt. This warrior is holding the tall bronze helmet of the fallen Hittite officer, E4.

3: Tjekker warlord
A bearded individual in the Medinet Habu reliefs is identified as a Tjekker chief. He wears a strange cap which, though uncrested, is reminiscent of some of the late Achaean helmets depicted on pottery, e.g. on side B of the famous 'Warriors Vase' from Mycenae. Note the use of two javelins, well attested by the Egyptian representations and by late Aegean pottery.

4: Hittite commander of the *Tuhuyeru*
This fallen Hittite leader is copied from warriors depicted in the reliefs of Yazilikaya. The scimitar-like single-edged sword for which he is grasping in vain is copied from a specimen of 1307–1275 BC, about 60cm (23.62in) long and considered to be of Hittite origin. It bears the incised name of the Assyrian King Adad-Nirari, a contemporary of Muwatalli II; its hilt was furnished with a flange for the attachment of the ivory grips.

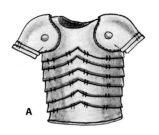
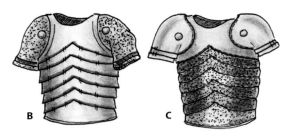
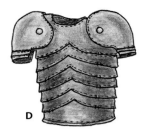

Hypothetical reconstructions of body armours worn by 'horned helmet' Sea Peoples from the Medinet Habu reliefs.
(A) Full bronze armour.
(B) Bronze cuirass worn over a garment of organic material.
(C) Composite cuirass of bronze and quilted material.
(D) Non-metallic corselet probably made of leather or other organic material.
(Drawings by Andrea Salimbeti)

OPPOSITE
Hypothetical reconstructions of body armours worn by 'feathered tiara' Sea Peoples from the Medinet Habu reliefs.
(A) Full bronze armour.
(B) Bronze cuirass with chest/back plates and lower bands, worn over a *kiton* of linen or other organic material.
(C) Composite cuirass of bronze and quilted material.
(D) Non-metallic corselet probably made of leather or other organic material.
(E) Full bronze cuirass, with throat protection between the shoulder-guards. The general design may be similar to some Achaean bronze armours attested or represented in Crete and the Greek mainland.
(F) Flexible corselet without sleeves or shoulder protection, probably of quilted material.
(G) Another flexible corselet, with shoulder and upper arm protection.
(Drawings by Andrea Salimbeti)

to about LHIIIC in Kallithea, Portes and Praisos-Foutoula. Bronze rings intended as part of the helmets' lower edge are also mentioned by Homer (VII, 12; X, 30; XI, 96), whose term *stefani*, i.e. 'crown-helmet', probably refers to this type. It is interesting to remember that Herodotus and Strabo also mention sailors from the Aegean coasts and Asia Minor being long known for their 'feathered crest' headgear.

In the Egyptian iconography of victory celebrations the Shekelesh and/or perhaps the Tjekker are shown wearing cloth headdresses. A Shekelesh prince is shown bearded, with a low turban or cap, wearing an armour composed of bands of organic material of different colours. The Denyen are sometimes illustrated with a low headgear whose shape recalls that of the 'tiara' helmet without the plumes. The clearly-identified leader of the Peleset wears a similar low turban, perhaps a sort of felt cap that could be worn under a helmet as padding.

Shields

In a relief from Luxor related to the battle of Kadesh, some Sea People warriors (probably Karkisa or Lukka) are shown bearing medium-sized round shields with two lateral cuts. Similar shields are also well attested in contemporary Hittite and Aegean representations. However, nearly all the Sea Peoples carry large or medium round shields with one or two handles, sometimes with bronze bosses attached. Protected by their shields, they hurl javelins from a short distance while attacking, and then draw their sword or dagger and fall upon the enemy. The bosses represented on some of the Sea Peoples' shields in reliefs from Medinet Habu might be associated with two specimens from Pyla-Kokkinokremos in Cyprus, dated to 1200–1100 BC; of 88mm (3.46in) diameter, these have a single central hole. For what it may be worth, two bronze statuettes representing warriors with small round shields have been found at Delos (dated LH IIIA-B, about 1350 BC) and at Enkomi (dated about 1200 BC). These show typical elements of both the Sea Peoples and the Near East, e.g. a horned helmet and a sickle sword.

A large circular or oval shield, carried by a warrior with the typical 'feathered tiara' headdress, is well represented in a domed seal from Enkomi, Cyprus, dated around 1190–1180 BC. The texture on the shield's external surface has been interpreted as a wicker structure; however, it has a large central boss, and we cannot exclude the possibility that the external surface of the shield might be made of sheet metal with embossed relief decorations, like the shields of Achilles and Agamemnon described by Homer.

Body armours

The first possible evidence of an Aegean mercenary wearing body armour comes from the Tel el-Amarna Papyrus, where one of the warriors seems to

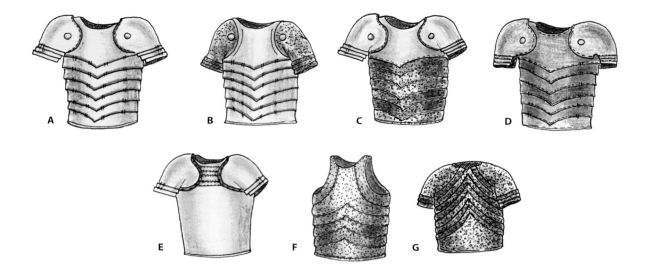

A · B · C · D

E · F · G

be equipped with a short-cropped corselet which leaves the stomach bare. These corselets are not represented in any other Egyptian images of soldiery, but are visible in some Aegean pottery representations, especially from Cyprus. The corselets shown on the papyrus have another relevant feature: a green copper-based paint has been used to suggest the presence of metal reinforcements at the corselet's neck, upper arms, and lower edge over the stomach (see Plate A3). Tablets in Linear B from Knossos (L693) attest the employment of linen tunics *(ki-to)* reinforced with bronze or copper fittings *(e-pi-ko-to-ni-ja)*. Short corselets with possible metallic neck collars and other fittings were still represented in several warrior statuettes from Sardinia dating from the 11th to 8th centuries BC.

Some of the Sherden mercenaries or royal bodyguards in Egyptian service are represented at the battle of Kadesh with the typical Egyptian quilted corselets, probably made of linen or thin leather and presumably constructed in padded layers.

The upper bodies of some warriors represented in the Medinet Habu reliefs are covered with corselets apparently made of wide bands of organic material or bronze, disposed in V or inverted-V shapes. Several hypotheses have been advanced about these banded so-called 'lobster-style' and 'ribbon' corselets; they were probably made of bronze, linen and leather, similar in their shapes but differing widely in details.

Many scholars (Yadin, Stillman and Tallis, Gorelik, Connolly, Andrikou, Cassola Guida, Snodgrass, etc) believe that the 'lobster armours' could have been of bronze in V-band arrangements. They appear to be similar in conception to one of the hypothetical reconstructions of the Achaean armour pieces found in Thebes and Nichoria, with narrow bands of plate around the body and rounded shoulder-pieces. The full bronze armour might have comprised chest-and-back plates, lower bands, and shoulder/upper arm defences. Some cuirasses with bronze chest-and-back plates and lower bands seem to be worn over a *kiton* of linen or other organic material. The composite cuirasses might also have had bronze chest-and-back plates and shoulder-pieces, with bands of quilted material around the lower torso. Similar V-banded corselets are also represented on warriors engraved on worked ivory from Cyprus and other Aegean localities. Other corselets

Aegean Group D spearhead, and Naue II Group A sword, from Enkomi, Cyprus, late 13th century BC. (Cyprus Museum, Nicosia; author's photos)

Late Bronze Age swords of Aegean/Anatolian type, published by Flinders Petrie. Various examples of contemporary daggers and swords found in Egypt are of non-Egyptian origin, and recall in general design those used in the Aegean and Anatolia, where the presence of the Sea Peoples is attested. (Author's collection)

Late 13th-century BC bronze sword from Ugarit, Syria, inscribed with the cartouche of the Pharaoh Merneptah. While it displays a general typological affinity with Central European examples, features such as the grooved blade and the royal cartouche imply Near Eastern production based on a foreign model. (ex Yadin; drawing by Andrea Salimbeti)

depicted might simply be made of bands of coloured leather, mainly of red, blue and light blue, arranged horizontally around the torso and abdomen.

Scale armour was also probably used. The shipwreck excavation at Uluburun near Kas on the southern Turkish coast has yielded a large bronze scale 30mm wide by 90mm long (roughly 1.25in x 3.5in). Other finds in this cargo ship, dated to about 1300 BC, include several Canaanite, Cypriot and Achaean manufactured goods as well as raw materials, weaponry and ceramics. A bronze scale 61mm (*c.*2.5in) long has also been found at the important Achaean settlement site of Pyla-Kokkinokremos in Cyprus, together with weapons, bronze objects and shield bosses. All these elements are dated to LHIIIC.

On Aegean-style krater fragments from Ugarit in Syria, dated to around 1200 BC, some warriors with horses seem to be equipped with a short cuirass possibly made of metal scales, plus neck protection, a conical helmet, a belt or *mitra*, greaves and a sword. While the artistic stylization allows several interpretations of the cuirass, a number of bronze scales also found in the same area may be significant.

Weapons:
Spears and javelins

Most of the Sea Peoples represented in the land battle on the Medinet Habu relief are equipped with long spears or medium-length javelins. Some warriors, as also attested by late Aegean pottery, are depicted fighting with two javelins. This is important: exactly at the end of the Bronze Age, warrior graves including two javelin heads begin to appear all over the Aegean area. The leaders of the Denyen and Tjekker shown being slaughtered by Ramesses III (north tower, east face of the temple) are in fact holding two javelins in their hands. The Egyptians' Sherden mercenaries shown in the same battle are armed with medium-long shafted spears having a foliate head.

Swords, daggers and maces

Most of the Sea People represented in Egyptian art are equipped with long or medium swords and sometimes with daggers. Among Near Eastern swords in the archaeological record is a specimen 90cm (35.43in) long found at Beth Dagan near Jaffa, Israel, dated to about 2000 BC, and probably similar in shape to some of the swords represented at Medinet Habu. Analysis of this huge blade has shown it to consist of almost pure copper with a small addition of arsenic. A 30cm (11.81in) dagger found in the same area shows a similar shape. About 30 similar swords dated to around 1600 BC have also been found in a remarkable cave grave near St Iroxi on the island of Sardinia, and these have the same material composition as the Beth Dagan specimen.

Elongated 'triangular' swords and daggers of Aegean style seem to have been the favourite weapons of several groups of Sea Peoples, e.g. the Sherden and Peleset. Some of the stout bronze swords of the Sea Peoples excavated

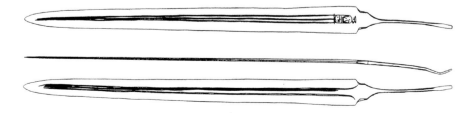

by Flinders Petrie are similar to some variants of the Naue II swords of Aegean origin. However, some scholars consider the long swords represented at Medinet Habu to be derived from the Achaean Type B attested in the Aegean area in 1600–*c*.1300 BC. The Egyptian version of these swords, represented in the painted tomb of Ramesses III, shows a gilded hilt. These swords were suspended by a baldric passing over the right shoulder, letting the sword hang in a diagonal position on the breast. The Egyptian representations are notable for the absence of scabbards, which are visible in contemporary Aegean representations and well attested by archaeology.

The war-staff or mace is depicted only in the hands of those Sea Peoples fighting as Egyptian mercenaries, being an Egyptian weapon. Its employment against Libyans and Aegean invaders is well attested in the Medinet Habu relief.

Bronze spearhead and dagger from the cemetery of Tel Es-Sa 'Idiyeh, Jordan, 1250–1150 BC. Traces of linen on the spear point indicate that the objects had either been wrapped before deposition, or had been incorporated into a tight binding around the deceased in the Egyptian manner. The custom of binding weapons in linen is already attested in the shaft graves of Mycenae as early as the 16th century BC. (British Museum; author's collection)

MILITARY ORGANIZATION

The land-battle and sea-battle scenes at Medinet Habu provide a wealth of information on the military styles of the Sea Peoples, even making it possible to extrapolate some hints as to their organization and tactics.

The reliefs depicting the land battle show Egyptian troops, chariots and auxiliaries fighting enemies who also use chariots, very similar in design to Egyptian ones. Ox *(zebu)*-drawn carts containing women and children are highlighted in an uppermost tier of the reliefs, chariots in the central tier, and only infantry in the lower – all indications of a relatively high degree of

Iron and bronze swords and dagger from the cemetery of Tel Es-Sa 'Idiyeh, 1250–1150 BC; chronologically this Jordanian site spans the transition between the Late Bronze and Iron ages. The presence of 'double *pithos*' in the burials may indicate the presence of a group of the Sea Peoples. (British Museum; author's collection)

Bronze bucket-shaped cylindrical helmet of c.1200 BC, found at Praisos-Foutoula in Crete; compare with Plate F1. A 'feathered' helmet with an unusually high 'tiara' also seems to be worn by a warrior represented on a relief at Medinet Habu – see right, with reconstruction. (ex Kanta; reconstruction by Andrea Salimbeti)

organization on the part of the Sea Peoples. Moreover, in the upper and lower left corners of the relief retreating warriors maintain their organization, being formed into ranks probably typical of their entire infantry before the Egyptian attack. Their host is composed of three main bodies:

(1) Non-combatant civilians, including women and children, are carried inside large square carts with two solid wheels, and with a single warrior as a guard. Four oxen are harnessed abreast; the carts are crude affairs built on wooden frames, possibly with woven-reed infill panels.

(2) Chariots using six-spoke wheels and pulled by two horses, very similar in design to Egyptian or Hittite chariots.

F · THE ISLAND CONSPIRACY: 'WAR OF THE EIGHTH YEAR', 1191/1178 BC

1: Peleset leader

One of the Peleset prisoners in the Medinet Habu reliefs seems to be a leader wearing a bronze helmet similar to a specimen from Crete; worn over an internal straw headpiece, this is about 16cm (6.30in) high, and decorated with 19 rows of embossing. From the top emerges a 'feathered' crest which we interpret as leather strips painted scarlet. The warrior wears a to-ra-ka cuirass in embossed bronze above bands of padded linen or other organic material. This method of wearing the naked sword slung on the breast is typical of some Aegean and Cypriot representations. An important sign of his rank is the trident-spear, symbol of dominion over the sea in reference to the god Po-se-i-ta-wo (Poseidon); this example is taken from a 12th-century BC find at the Achaean settlement of Hala Sultan Tekke in Cyprus. Similar tridents continued to be symbols of command in the nearby later Philistine culture of present-day Israel, and among the Sardinians (sculpture from Nurdole di Orani) and Etruscans (bronze specimen from Vetulonia).

2: Sherden leader

This chief of the 'Sea Sherden', copied from the Medinet Habu sea-battle relief, wears a helmet of a type also visible on a statuette from Cyprus, in bronze with a central disc and two ivory side-horns. His to-ra-ka is entirely of embossed bronze, again with a breastplate above inverted-V bands. The gold pectoral medallion and the two bronze bracelets are no doubt signs of status.

3: Shekelesh leader

Again from the Medinet Habu representations, he wears a plain, low-profile cap presumably of hardened leather. His leather or fabric body armour shows eight bands in alternating colours; this type of protection was probably fastened down the back. His typical Near Eastern 'sickle sword' is a specimen from Gezer, entirely in bronze and 70cm (27.56in) in length. Prisoners identified as Tjekker in the Medinet Habu reliefs are characterized by a medallion on the chest; this is also associated with the Shekelesh, and might have been distinctive of these ethnic groups.

Detail of the land battle between the Egyptians and the Sea People during Ramesses III's campaigns. This scene from the upper tier of the Medinet Habu reliefs shows Aegean warriors fighting on a solid-wheeled ox-cart, to defend their women and children from Egyptian spearmen wearing *klaft* headdress. (ex Epigraphic Survey, Egyptian Museum Library, Turin)

Several pole-sockets ending in a 'crook' tip, dating from the late 13th century BC, have been found in Cyprus. Some scholars relate these to the several Homeric descriptions of leaders as 'shepherds' of their people. The crook-sceptre in Egypt was a symbol of royal or divine power; it is also shown in the hands of official visitors, perhaps because they are, or represent, leaders. (From Enkomi, Cyprus Museum, Nicosia, author's photo)

(3) Infantrymen armed with a pair of long spears or javelins, who sometimes seem to be arrayed in small 'proto-phalanxes' of four or more men. Some of them carry long straight swords, some only a short dagger. It is interesting to recall here the proto-phalanxes described by Homer for the Achaeans, and the proto-phalanx of Minoan warriors depicted in the Thera frescoes (see Osprey Warrior 167, *Early Aegean Warrior 5000–1450 BC*).

In the land-battle representation the Peleset or other Sea Peoples are shown fighting from Near Eastern-style chariots equipped with lateral quivers for bow and arrows. Interestingly, however, the warriors on the chariots are armed only with spears and shields like most Aegean chariot troops, instead of the bows that were typical of Near Eastern chariot crews.

Leadership

Some scholars have argued a lack of centralized leadership from the apparent absence of Sea Peoples' leaders in the Egyptian sources. However, the Egyptians refer (in general terms) to 'leaders' and 'great ones' of the Sea Peoples, and the tower of Medinet Habu bears emblematic representations of foreigners most of whom are identified as political and military leaders. The representatives of the Tjekker and Peleset are also specifically identified as 'great ones' – a kind of leadership perhaps associated more with mobile groups like the Sea Peoples (the same title is also applied to leaders of the Shasu, a nomadic people of Canaan). The organized military initiatives by the Sea Peoples suggest that, even if confederated, they had developed military and political leadership to a substantial degree. Major military expeditions on both land and sea such as those against the Egyptians would have required, if not a single 'commander-in-chief', then at least commanders for each group acting in a degree of co-ordination with each other.

In the sea-battle reliefs we have a further possible representation of Sea Peoples' leaders, indicated by the manacles that they wear after capture. The manacle was a relatively comfortable and efficient means of restraint;

Detail from Medinet Habu showing (right) a high-ranking prisoner wearing a 'feathered' headdress and with his wrists confined by fish-shaped manacles. The same figure appears in another scene showing prisoners being assigned to royal or temple servitude. (ex Epigraphic Survey, Egyptian Museum Library, Turin)

for example, all the Sea Peoples warriors captured during the sea battle are shown as manacled, seated in the Egyptian ships. Once on shore and being prepared for presentation to the pharaoh, prisoners have their manacles removed, and their arms are cruelly forced together and tied behind their backs, or even above their heads (as was typical during such ceremonies – see Plate C2). However, some of prisoners continue to wear the more comfortable and less degrading manacles, perhaps indicating a recognition of special status; for example, Mesher, son of Kepher, leader of the Meshwesh, is treated in this way. Moreover, these manacles are uniquely lion- or fish-shaped (while all the others are plain), emblematic of pharaonic power and hence of the captives' subordination to the pharaoh. The men thus represented might be the senior leaders of the Sea Peoples.

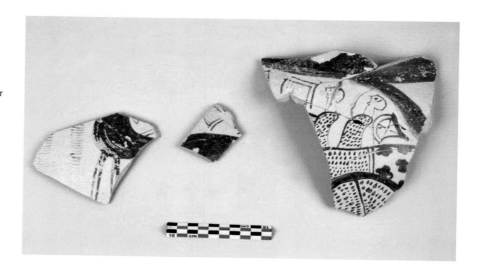

Late Bronze Age Aegean pottery from Gibala, Syria. An Aegean-style chariot carrying two possibly bow-armed warriors is represented on this fragment from near Ugarit, recovered in a destruction layer precisely carbon-dated to between 1220 and 1180 BC. These finds, and several associated arrow- or small javelin-heads, have been attributed to the invasion by the Sea Peoples. (Courtesy Dr David Kaniewsky, Tel Dweini Project)

TACTICS

War chariots

The Sea Peoples' war chariots in the land-battle relief from Medinet Habu are depicted with a crew of three, a driver and two fighting men, while the Egyptians have only one or occasionally two. They are armed only with javelins or spears in Late Aegean style. From the tactical point of view, the

Detail from the Medinet Habu reliefs showing Ramesses III's land battle against the Sea Peoples; Aegean spearmen or javelineers are shown in chariots with six-spoke wheels. (ex Epigraphic Survey, Egyptian Museum Library, Turin)

Egyptian reliefs show us that some warriors probably specialized in the protection of the chariots and their horse-teams – an important element of 'connection' between the two main elements of Late Bronze Age armies, the cavalry and infantry. The 'running warriors' protected the chariots both when they were deployed against infantry ranks and against other chariots. In the former case, at the moment of penetrating the enemy ranks there was a high risk of chariot crews being dismounted and attacked from several directions; and when fighting against enemy chariots the 'running warriors' went into action against their crews in advance. Some Sherden mercenaries in Egyptian service may also have specialized in such tactics.

An ivory gaming box from Enkomi, Cyprus (see photograph, page 23) shows a chariot with a mix of Aegean/Anatolian features; it has six-spoke wheels, and bears the driver and a bow-armed warrior with a scale cuirass. Another hunter-warrior running near the chariot is armed with an axe, and wears the typical Sea Peoples 'feathered' headdress.

Siege warfare

One possible hypothesis for the destruction of Troy VII is that the city was besieged and sacked in around 1180 BC by a coalition of the Sea Peoples mainly formed by Aegean Greeks. The possible siege tactics can be partly deduced from the Homeric poems, which clearly describe the techniques typical of the Late Bronze Age.

The attackers arrived in their ships and established a base camp protected by a fortification; they knew that a siege might be prolonged, and that they

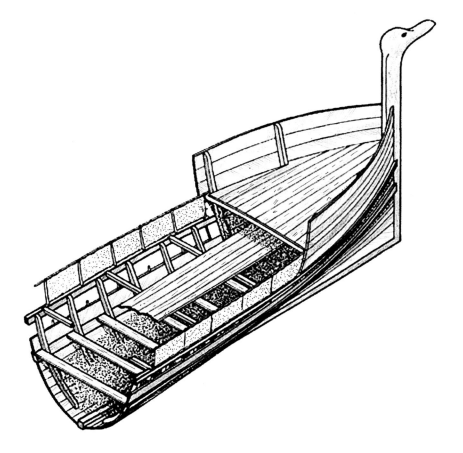

Isometric reconstruction of the bow of a Sea Peoples ship. Some elements are deduced from the positions of the corpses on one of the Peleset ships represented in the Medinet Habu relief. The presence of a bulwark to protect rowers, and the close similarity with Aegean ships, supports the idea that the Sea Peoples had oarsmen, but that they were not represented in the Medinet Habu relief because in confined waters the oars were shipped and stowed. (ex F.M. Hocker; drawing by Andrea Salimbeti)

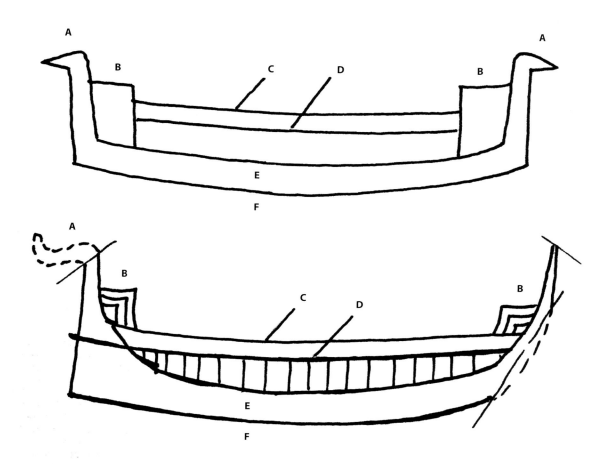

Comparisons of a Sea Peoples ship represented in the Medinet Habu temple relief, and an Achaean Greek ship depicted at Kynos. Common elements are the 'bird's-head' prow and stern (A), the two raised platforms at bow and stern (B), bulwarks to protect rowers (C, D), and the wooden hull (gunwale E, keel F). This comparison suggests a significant interconnection between the Achaeans and the Sea Peoples, which is supported by other aspects of material culture. (ex F.M. Hocker; drawings by Andrea Salimbeti)

must defend themselves and their beached ships from counter-attacks. Unlike armies of later ages they did not have the numbers or the means to completely cut off the defenders from resupply or movement. To prevent the city receiving help, and to feed themselves, the attackers conducted a series of raids against neighbouring towns, as described in Hittite tablets, and the clashes that these occasioned might develop into major battles. Neither did they have sophisticated siege engines, and when groups of warriors attempted to climb the walls they did so with bare hands or simple ladders, while the defenders shot arrows and dropped stones.

Naval warfare and seaborne raids

From Cypriot, Hittite and Egyptian documents we learn of the methods employed by the Sea Peoples during their naval raids. They seem to have avoided direct confrontation at sea when possible. When they were forced to fight a sea battle they fared poorly, as is evident from their naval engagements against the Hittites under Suppiluliuma II: 'I, Suppiluliuma II the Great King, immediately crossed [reached?] the sea. The ships of Alashiya [Cypriot Sea Peoples] met me in battle at sea three times, and I smote them; I seized the ships and set fire to them on the sea.' The Sea Peoples were similarly unsuccessful against Egyptian fleets under Ramesses II and Ramesses III.

Instead these maritime marauders appear to have preferred hit-and-run raids, falling upon coastal communities to pillage and burn and then escaping

before the local military force could respond effectively. They seem to have been constantly on the move, and hard to catch; their incessant evasive movements would have led them to appear to the other Mediterranean cultures as 'peoples of the sea' who 'live on their ships'. They seem to have operated in small flotillas of between seven and 20 ships, at least during the period when they were active in the north-east Mediterranean prior to their arrival on the coast of Egypt. These modest numbers are interesting when contrasted with the massive, 150-ship fleet that Ugarit was asked to supply.

The clearest representations of ships associated with the Sea Peoples are the five vessels carved on the temple walls at Medinet Habu. In this scene both the possible Sherden and Peleset ships are well represented; they are of a uniform type, with a single mast with a crow's-nest, and a high prow and stern terminating in so-called 'duck's-head' carvings. The Sea Peoples' vessels have no visible oars (they were probably stowed inside the ships, since in this scenario they were already anchored inside a bay), and only the raised sail is shown. The ships are steered by means of a large paddle. This type of vessel shows close similarity with the ship depicted on a stirrup jar from Skyros and on a krater sherd from Tiryns (both dated LHIIIC); some Central European Urnfield ornaments represent double bird's-headed boats, as do Early Iron Age ship models from Sardinia.

The type of ship used is believed to offer crucial evidence for the identity of the Sea Peoples and for the aim of their attacks. According to some scholars, these vessels find their best parallel in Achaean oared galleys, the most detailed example being the representation on a krater from Kynos (by Dr Wedde's classification, Type V of Achaean galleys). While providing a fighting platform at sea, it was also designed to transport soldiers and plunder. Because this kind of oared ship needed a full rowing crew for operations, and because it was only partially decked, the number of passengers or amount of cargo that could be carried was rather limited – perhaps only ten or so men in addition to rowers and other crew, with no extra space for cargo. This, combined with the fact that only male warriors

The army of Ramesses III on the march; the Egyptian artist has clearly suggested its mixed character, showing troops of various nationalities. After a first rank of native Egyptians with 'tombstone' shields (left), we can make out a mixed rank of Sea Peoples mercenaries, including Sherden wearing their horns-and-disc helmets alternating with warriors wearing the 'feathered' headdress associated with the Peleset; they carry single spears and long swords. Behind them (right) are a rank of bearded men wearing a back-swept headdress – perhaps Tjekker or Shekelesh? – and carrying pairs of javelins and short, wavy-bladed swords. (ex Epigraphic Survey, Egyptian Museum Library, Turin)

appear in the Medinet Habu scene, clearly indicates a force of a different character than the 'colonization' party shown in the land-battle relief – an all-male raiding force such as that which attacked Ugarit, and recalling Odysseus's nine-ship raid on Egypt (*Od.* 14: 245–9).

An exhaustive analysis of the Sea Peoples' ships has been made by Shelley Wachsmann of the Institute of Nautical Archaeology, College Station, Texas. The vessels represented at Medinet Habu, carrying about 30 fighters each, have no cut-water, but vertical stem and stern posts topped with bird heads similar to some Aegean ships represented on LHIIIC pottery. Two structures for fighting purposes are erected above the deck level, while a rail running round the sides of the vessel protects the rowers. A curved upper yard hangs from the single mast, which terminates at the top in a crow's-nest for a look-out. Wachsmann proposes the presence of additional fighting decks on these ships, basing this upon analysis of the reliefs.

The appearance of a flotilla of five ship images in the Medinet Habu reliefs is misleading, as all five of them are demonstrably taken from a single

Detail of the land battle against the Sea People: the massacre of the invaders. At upper right, note the very clearly depicted inverted-V pattern of body armour, and the sword slung across the chest. At bottom right, the defeated javelineer invaders retreat from the field apparently in orderly ranks. (ex Epigraphic Survey, Egyptian Museum Library, Turin)

prototype. A review of the depictions of similar ships in the Aegean tradition shows that, even if remarkably similar, no two are virtually identical as is the case of the Medinet Habu vessels, and the range of ships in the invading fleet was probably far more diverse than shown in the reliefs. Similarly, only one type of Egyptian ship is represented, four times, while the related inscription mentions three different types of ships as having taken part. There can be no doubt that the Egyptian artists recorded a single foreign ship five times, nor that this depiction was based on actual observation. We know from several sources that artists accompanied military expeditions as well as trading ventures. Presumably, in the aftermath of the battle, the artist made a sketch study of single vessels from each side for use in creating the naval battle scene.

Mixed group of Sea Peoples mercenaries in fierce and victorious combat with Libyans – compare with Plate G. The Egyptian iconographic sources usually (but not invariably) depict the Sea Peoples as beardless, in contrast with, e.g., Libyans and Levantine peoples. In the Medinet Habu reliefs the Sea Peoples are shown with round shields, spears, javelins, swords or daggers, but never with bows. (ex Epigraphic Survey, Egyptian Museum Library, Turin)

'THE WAR OF THE EIGHTH YEAR', 1191 or 1184 BC

The invasion

The royal speech of Usermare Meryamun Ramesses (Ramesses III), engraved in hieroglyphics, records the last attempted invasion of Egypt by the Sea Peoples. It is worth quoting several passages from this primary source, although its interpretation is not always straightforward:

'The Northerners made a conspiracy in their islands. All at once the lands were removed and scattered in the fray. Not one stood before their hands, from Hatti, Kode, Carchemish, Arzawa, Alashiya, they were wasted. [They set up] a camp in one place in Amurru. They desolated his people and his land like that which is not [i.e. as if it had never existed].… Their confederation was Peleset, Tjekker, Shekelesh, Denyen, and Weshesh. [These] lands were united, and they laid their hands upon the lands to the very Circle of the Earth. Their hearts were confident, full of their plans, but a net was prepared for them…'. The Papyrus Harris gives the confederate Sea Peoples as the Peleset, Tjekker/Sikila (Shekelesh?), Denyen, Weshesh and Sherden.

Egyptian warriors attacking Sea Peoples during the sea battle. In this interesting detail of an Egyptian officer striking a Peleset (?) warrior with a mace, the fallen 'Northerner' seems to wear a light fabric corselet without shoulder protection; compare with reconstructions on page 37, image F. (ex Epigraphic Survey, Egyptian Museum Library, Turin)

The texts provide the precise date of the conflict – Year 8 of the reign of the pharaoh – and also explain that the invasion of Egypt by the Sea Peoples was only the last phase in successive waves of destruction that had disturbed most of the Late Bronze Age. The general direction of this invasion was probably from the area of the Aegean and southern Anatolia towards Egypt. Two main bodies of invaders were on the move, according to a pre-established plan; one group proceeded across Anatolia from the north-west towards the south-east, the other by both land and sea down the coasts from south-west Anatolia. Originally some scholars translated the Egyptian sources as speaking of the land of the Sea Peoples as 'islands in the middle of the sea' (specifically for the Danuna), taking this to refer to populations coming directly from the Aegean islands (Crete and/or the Achaean colonies in

G MERCENARIES DEFEATING LIBYANS

Of particular importance among the reliefs at Medinet Habu is one depicting a mixed group of Sea Peoples mercenaries among Egyptian forces who are fiercely slaughtering Libyans – either in Ramesses III's Year 8, or perhaps in his subsequent campaign of Year 11? They include Sherden wearing helmets topped with the disc-and-horns (1 & 4); and probably Peleset or Denyen/Danuna with their 'feather'-topped helmets (2 & 3). These 'tiara' headpieces had various degrees of face and neck protection, here probably made of leather scales. In the original relief from which these warriors are copied, details remain of round shields with small metal studs; these are similar to shields attested in some Late Bronze Age Achaean graves and represented on LHIIIC pottery. The mercenaries' weapons are iron-headed spears and bronze swords.

The basic garment of Labu warriors (5) was just a phallus-sheath of leather attached to a waist belt, but cloaks were worn that passed under the left arm and were tied up on the right shoulder. These might be made of bull-hide, or (perhaps in the case of leaders) from the pelts of animals such as giraffe or lion. The feather plume worn in the hair was considered important, and indicated different tribes and a man's status within them. The Libyans often decorated their bodies with tattoos or painting.

This image from the Medinet Habu sea-battle relief shows Sherden warriors. Note the large shield, horned helmet lacking a central disc and with flared-down neck-guard, javelins, and what seems (by comparison of both figures) to be the so-called 'lobster' cuirass – of bronze, with large rounded shoulder-guards above inverted-V bands around the torso. The two diagonal lines across the inside of the shield are not parts of it, but ropes from the ship's rigging. (ex Epigraphic Survey, Egyptian Museum Library, Turin)

Cyprus). Transliteration of Ramesses III's original text should be read as invaders who 'came from their countries and from the islands in the middle of the Great Green'. Various interpretations have been argued, citing different historical uses of this latter term.

For a long time it was believed that it simply referred to the Mediterranean Sea, and that at least during the 18th Dynasty the phrase 'islands in the middle of the Great Green' *(iww ḥryw ib nw w3d wr)* should be understood as the islands and coasts of the Aegean, possibly even the Greek mainland. In the Decree of Canopus it refers to Cyprus, and on the Rosetta Stone *w3d wr* is translated in Greek as τήν θάλασσαν. Conversely, in an older inscription in Wadi Hammamat Hénu, from Year 8 of Montuhotep III (about 2006 BC), it is used to indicate the Red Sea, and this use continues until the 18th Dynasty. Finally, use of this term in reference to the Nile, its waters and the Delta (green, as opposed to the surrounding deserts) dates back at least to the 5th Dynasty reign of Niuserra. Its specific meaning has varied from time to time, while always maintaining an idea of relative 'centrality'; with regard to the Delta, it has been used to mean the islands located in its centre. Recent discoveries about the topography of the main lagoon city of the Delta, Avaris (Tel el-Dab'a) are an example of how different locations could legitimately be described as 'islands in the middle of the Great Green'. With regard to the Sea Peoples, this interpretation allows the hypothesis that some of the invaders established a base camp among the islands in the Delta.

To return to the Egyptian records of the War of the Eighth Year: they tell us that the ancient kingdoms of Sapalulu and Khâtusaru crumbled to pieces under the shock of invasion, and that Ugarit on the Syrian coast was

destroyed in about 1193 BC. It is noteworthy that in the Ugarit sources the invaders are called 'the Shikala who live on the ships'. Shortly afterwards Hattusa was also sacked, and Cyprus (Alashiya) ravaged, perhaps by a civil war in which the Sea Peoples were involved. The invaders spread over the valley of the Orontes, burning and devastating the countryside. A possible reference to scorched-earth tactics can be found in the records: 'They came with fire prepared before them, forward to Egypt'. The Hittite vassal state of Amurru (Amor), located close to the border of the Egyptian empire, was sacked, and the invaders constructed there a camp for their women and their booty. Some of their predatory bands, having ravaged the Bekâa Valley, attacked the subjects of the pharaoh, and their chiefs dreamed of an invasion of Egypt itself. Archaeology offers evidence that in exactly this period the cities of the southern coast of Canaan were ravaged by the Philistines. An inscription from Medinet Habu confirms that the Philistines were already in possession of at least one city, indicating that the occupation of the pentapolis by the Peleset/Philistines began in this period.

The land battle

According to the Egyptian sources, these populations made concerted attacks by land and by sea, and two distinct battles are illustrated in the sculptural reliefs. Based on the order of the inscriptions and images along the wall of Medinet Habu, it appears that the 'land battle of Djahi' (Zahi) occurred first. Ramesses ordered a massive mobilization in order to stop the invaders' march towards Egypt. He crossed the frontier with Canaan and advanced by forced marches to attack the enemy's camp. His aim was presumably to contain the

From the composition of the scene and his posture of command, the central figure braving a shower of arrows here may be a ship's captain of the Sea Peoples. The carved lines suggest a full Aegean-style cuirass, probably of bronze, with upper chest/throat protection showing between the large rounded shoulder-guards. His short sword might be identified with the Aegean Type H classification. (ex Epigraphic Survey, Egyptian Museum Library, Turin)

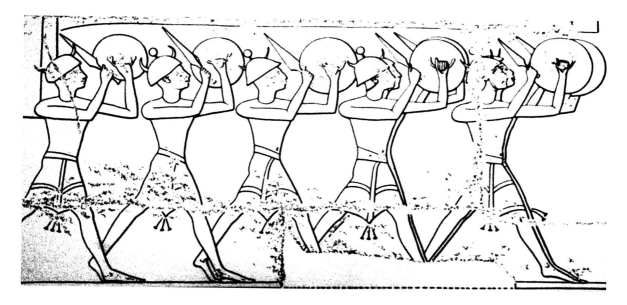

After defeating them in Egypt, Ramesses III marched north to retake the fortress of Amor previously captured by the Sea Peoples. His army included these Sherden mercenaries; they are depicted with simple helmets fitted with horns and discs; Aegean/Anatolian kilts; small bucklers with single central grips; and short swords or daggers of a shape generally corresponding with bronze specimens found in the Aegean, Anatolia and the Near East. (ex Epigraphic Survey, Egyptian Museum Library, Turin)

attempted conquest of Canaan by the Sea Peoples who had already seized or were attacking its coastal towns. He encountered the invaders somewhere not far beyond the Egyptian frontier, probably near the coast: 'His Majesty sets out for Zahi... to crush every enemy... The charioteers selected from among the most rapid warriors... Their horses were quivering in their every limb, ready to crush the [foreign] countries under their feet... Those who reached my boundary, their seed is not; the period of their soul has been fixed forever'.

In the land-battle scenes the Sea Peoples and Egyptians are represented in chaotic combat, while the pharaoh shoots arrows against the enemy. The Egyptians attack with their chariots and swordsmen, the Sea Peoples resist with javelins; they are shown falling, pierced by many arrows shot by chariot crews, while the Egyptian infantry and their mercenaries mercilessly kill warriors, women and children in a bloody onslaught. The pharaoh carried off from the field, in addition to the treasures of the confederate tribes, some of the carts which had been used for the transport of their families. The survivors of the Sea Peoples made their way hastily north-west towards the sea in order to reach the support of their ships, while followed by the victorious Egyptians.

H | SEA PEOPLES IN SARDINIA, c.1100 BC

1: Sherden warrior

This figure, copied from a Sardinian statuette, has a horned helmet with a median ridge rising in two peaks, a diadem-shaped bronze headband, and leather face protection here hanging loose. His padded corselet, made of some organic material, is composed of vertical strips with two large shoulder-guards recalling an Aegean type of body armour, with bronze tassets resembling Hellenic types. He carries a small buckler, and a long thrusting-sword with a curved hilt.

2: Peleset warrior

Here we choose to reconstruct the bronze 'tiara' helmet with actual feather plumes. The Aegean-style armour may attest the contemporary presence on this western Mediterranean island of different groups of Sea Peoples. The leather cuirass is reinforced with metal bosses, and has large shoulder- and collar-pieces as additional protection. Like his Aegean ancestors, this man is wearing short coloured trousers. Note his long sword, from Decimo Putzu; the weapons found in the cave grave near St Iroxi have a triangular blade with double middle ribs, giving a precise comparison with blades found in the area of El-Argar. The hilt, of some organic material, was fixed by rivets.

3: Sardinian (Sardian) woman

Her colourful dress, typically Aegean in style, is copied from a bronze statuette from Teti-Albini near Nuoro. In the background is a masonry-built *nuraghe* tower of the type found in Sardinia.

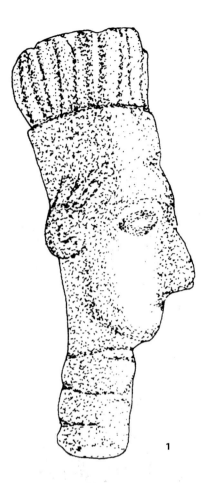

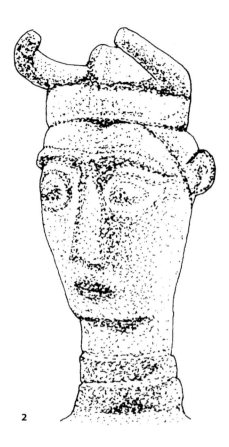

Heads of warrior statuettes from Sardinia, 1100–1000 BC; compare with Plate H. The 'feathered' headdress comes from a find at Ala dei Sardi, the horned one from Decimo Putzu. (Museo Archeologico Nazionale, Cagliari; ex Lilliu, drawings by Andrea Salimbeti)

The sea battle

Subsequently, the Sea Peoples' fleet approached the Nile Delta, and the pharaoh marched quickly back to face it. The huge naval clash, one of the first of its scale recorded in history, has been located in widely different possible places by various scholars. For some (e.g. Chabas), it took place close to the Delta, at the mouth of the eastern branch near Pelusium; for others, perhaps off Rafah in the present-day Gaza Strip, or Nahr el-Kelb (Van Muller), or as far north as Magadil in Lebanon (Maspero). The fact that the Egyptians were able to mobilize a great number of troops and ships seems to point towards the first hypothesis, which is supported by the Papyrus Harris: '...before the river-mouths'. A naval attack on the mouth of the Pelusiac branch of the Nile would threaten the pharaoh's northern cities and would logically provoke a massive Egyptian response.

According to Maspero, Ramesses rejoined his ships probably at Jaffa, and sailed to engage the enemy fleet. The Sea Peoples were encamped on the level shore at the head of a bay wide enough to offer to their ships sufficient space to manoeuvre; but they had dropped anchor, unaware of the presence of the Egyptian forces nearby. The latter consisted of both warships, and infantry stationed on the shore commanded by Ramesses himself. The pharaoh drove the enemy foot-soldiers into the water at the same moment that his admirals attacked the combined enemy fleet. Both sides used sails, but the Egyptian oars were fully deployed so they were able to manoeuvre, while those of the

Sea Peoples were stowed. The absence of oars in the representation of the Sea Peoples' ships suggests that they have been caught by surprise in inshore waters, and the accompanying texts seem to describe such a situation: 'The countries which came from their isles... advanced to Egypt, their hearts relying upon their arms. The net was made ready for them, to ensnare them. Entering stealthily into the harbour-mouth, they fell into it. Caught in their place, they were dispatched and their bodies stripped...'.

The Egyptian ships were rowed in close to the enemy vessels. Relying on their hand-to-hand combat superiority, the Sea Peoples came armed only with close-combat weapons, and this was a fatal mistake. Despite their armour the composite bows of the Egyptians slaughtered them before they could get to hand-to-hand range. From crow's-nests on the Egyptian ships slingers launched missiles down; other seamen used boarding-pikes at the bow to fend off enemy warriors as the vessels collided. Then the Egyptians boarded the enemy ships, attacking the already weakened crews. Egyptian sailors positioned in the prow threw grappling hooks into the enemy's rigging. Armed with thrusting spears and javelins, and supported by archers and slingers, the Egyptians boarded the Sea Peoples' vessels in a fierce mêlée. Some of the Aegean galleys capsized and sank when Egyptian ships rammed them with their sharp prows, and many warriors drowned; others were taken prisoner and chained aboard ship. The Sea Peoples were forced towards the shore, only to be picked off by the massed archers commanded by Ramesses and his sons. The invaders perished in the surf, or were taken prisoner as they emerged from the water, to be sent to join the line of captives. Egyptian officers seized each prisoner's wrist and pressed against his right shoulder a branding-iron heated in a brazier of live coals. This tool bore the name of the pharaoh, showing that the branded captives were now his slaves (Papyrus Harris, 77, 5–6: '...branded, made into slaves and stamped with my name...'). The leaders of the Sea Peoples and of other nations involved in their coalition were presented in chains in front of the god Amon-Re by the triumphant Pharaoh Ramesses III:

'As for those who had assembled before them on the sea, the full flame was in their front, before the river-mouths, and a wall of metal upon the shore surrounded them. They were dragged, overturned, and laid low upon the beach; slain and made heaps from stern to bow of their galleys, while all their things were cast upon the water. [Thus] I turned back the waters to remember Egypt; when they mention my name in their land, may it consume them... I permit not the countries to see the boundaries of Egypt... As for the Nine Bows, I have taken away their land and their boundaries; they are added to mine. Their chiefs and their people [come] to me with praise...'.

In the Papyrus Harris, Ramesses boasts that 'I extended the frontiers of Egypt and overthrew those who had attacked them from their lands. I slew the Denyen in their islands, while the Tjekker and the Philistines were made ashes. The Sherden and Weshesh of the Sea were made not-existent, captured all together and brought in captivity to Egypt, like the sands of the shore.'

Egyptian caricature doll found on the island of Malta, and probably representing a Philistine. (Drawing courtesy Dr Andrei Negin)

Bronze mask probably representing a horned warrior or divinity of the Sea Peoples, c.1400–1150 BC, from an unknown Near Eastern site. Masks of this sort were also produced in pottery, and were perhaps used as inserts on large wooden statues. This example has a hole high on either side which may have held two horns, to represent a Sherden warrior. The general features of this mask are reminiscent of warriors represented in bronze statuettes from Sardinia. (British Museum; author's collection)

Aftermath

A fast warship carried the Egyptian standard north along the coast as far as the regions of the Orontes and Saros. The land troops, following on the heels of the defeated enemy, succeeded in reaching the plains of the Euphrates. For a short time southern Syria returned to Egyptian rule.

The invading forces had been crushed in battle; but it is possible that Egyptian victory in this campaign was not total, since it was followed by treaties. The Egyptians agreed to settle some groups of invaders in Canaan, or to recognize them in territories they had already won before the battle of Zahi. Some would serve as mercenaries, being stationed as frontier garrisons along the Fertile Crescent, including the Philistines who settled in the Shephelah on the southern coastal plain of Palestine (Tel Beith Mirsim, Tel Qasile). In the Papyrus Harris, Ramesses III claims that: 'Their military classes were as numerous as a hundred thousand. I assigned tributes for them all with clothing and provisions from treasuries and granaries every year... [I] settled them in strongholds, bound in my name.' Some captives participated, as Egyptian mercenaries, in the campaign against the Libyans in Year 11 of his reign.

Although Ramesses III gives the impression that he has completely eradicated the Sea Peoples, they remained a major threat in the Mediterranean. Their defeat prevented them from conquering Egypt itself, but the Egyptians were still incapable of expelling them from Canaan completely. Egyptian suzerainty was nominally still strong in inland Canaan until the time of Ramesses IV, but the garrisons in Canaan probably represented an unavoidable Egyptian recognition of the conquests achieved by the Philistines.

*   *   *

Some scholars suggest that the land and sea battles won by Ramesses III were not single events, but represent a series of relatively smaller encounters between the Sea Peoples and Egyptian forces, or a 'global impression' of many similar clashes of the kind seen in the Papyrus Harris condensed into a single narrative of pharaonic victory. They support this interpretation by the inconsistencies between some of the named Sea Peoples mentioned in the Medinet Habu inscriptions and the Papyrus Harris, and the people actually shown in the reliefs (e.g., the Sherden are probably shown in the naval-battle relief but are not mentioned in the inscription of Year 8 – though their chief is shown elsewhere in the Medinet Habu carvings, and they are mentioned again in Papyrus Harris as 'the Sherden and the Weshesh of the Sea'). These scholars offer evidence of recurring maritime raids on Egypt during the 13th and 12th centuries BC, thus suggesting that the campaign of Year 8 may not have been an isolated event. In support of this they offer the depiction of warriors with 'feathered' headdress already in Egyptian service against Libyans and Nubians in the campaigns of the pharaoh's Year 5.

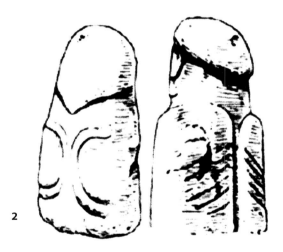

Statue-menhirs from Cauria (1) and Scalsa Murta (2), southern Corsica, carbon-dated to c.1400–1000 BC with a 200-year margin of error. These extraordinary menhirs possibly recall the first raids by Sea Peoples into the western Mediterranean. The added horns (1) are reconstructed on the basis of shallow holes in some of the menhirs; note also the long swords hanging on the chests. The carved lines on (2) might suggest a 'lobster' cuirass with large shoulder-guards above slanting bands. (Drawings by Andrea Salimbeti)

Fallen warriors from the Medinet Habu sea-battle scene. The central figure has a carefully-rendered zig-zag pattern on the band of his 'tiara' helmet; and note at right the suggestion of the large shoulder-guards and slanted rib-armour bands of a bronze cuirass, termed by some scholars as 'lobster-type' armour. (ex Epigraphic Survey, Egyptian Museum Library, Turin)

However, there is nothing remarkable in the idea that some Sea Peoples wearing this headgear had reached Egypt as prisoners and/or mercenaries before Year 5. The date is too late for them to have been prisoners taken during the Libyan campaigns of Merneptah; but the reputation of Anatolian and Aegean mercenaries was already well known, and their ancestors had previously served in Egyptian armies. It is more credible that among various successive clashes between the Egyptians and sea-raiders two decisive engagements, one on land and one at sea, did indeed take place.

BIBLIOGRAPHY

anon, *The Epigraphic Survey, Medinet Habu, Vols I & II, Earlier Historical Records of Ramses III, OIP 8 & OIP 9* (Chicago University Press, 1930 & 1932)

anon, *The Epigraphic Survey, Medinet Habu VIII, The Eastern High Gate, OIP 94* (Chicago University Press, 1970)

Aruz, J., Benzel, K. & Evans, J., *Beyond Babylon – Art, Trade and Diplomacy in the Second Millennium BC* (New York, 2008)

Basch, L. & Artzy, M., 'Ship Graffiti at Kition', in Karageorghis, V. & Demas, M., *Pyla-Kokkinokremos: A Late 13th-Century BC Fortified Settlement in Cyprus*; and 'The Pre-Phoenician Levels: Areas I and II', in *Excavations at Kition, Cyprus, Vol 5* (Nicosia; Dept of Antiquities, Cyprus, 1984 & 1985)

Basedow, M., *Besik-Tepe: Das spatbronzezeitliche Graberfeld, Studia Troica Monographien 1,* (Mainz, 2000)

Beckman, G.M., Bryce, T.R. & Cline, E., *The Ahhiyawa Text* (Atlanta, 2011)

Borchhardt, J., *Homerische Helme* (Mainz am Rhein, 1972)

Cabriolu, M., *Il popolo Shardana* (Cagliari, 2010)

Cavillier, G., *Gli Shardana nell'Egitto Ramesside* (Oxford, 2005)

Colleen, M., 'The Great Karnak Inscription of Merneptah: Grand Strategy in the 13th Century BC', in *Yale Egyptological Studies 3* (New Haven, 2003)

D'Amato, R. & Salimbeti, A., *Bronze Age Greek Warrior 1600–1100 BC,* Warrior No.153 (Oxford, 2010)

D'Amato, R. & Salimbeti, A., 'The War of the Eighth Year – The Battle of the Delta', in *Ancient Warfare, IV* (2010)

De Montis, A., *Il popolo di bronzo* (Cagliari, 2005)

Dothan, T. & Dothan, M., *People of the Sea: The Search for the Philistines* (New York, 1992)

Drews, R., 'Oxcarts, ships and migration theories', in *Journal of Near Eastern Studies, Vol. 59, No. 3* (July 2000)

Eisenlohr, A., *Der große Papyrus Harris, ein wichtiger Beitrag zur ägyptischen Geschichte, ein 3000 Jahr altes Zeugniss für die mosaische Religionsstiftung enthaltend* (Leipzig (1872)

Emanuel, J.P., 'Šrdn from the Sea: the Arrival, Integration and Acculturation of a Sea People', in *Journal of Ancient Egyptian Interconnections, 5* (2013)

Faucounau, J., *Les Peuples de la Mer et leur histoire* (Paris, 2003)

Garcia, A.F., 'La batalla del Nilo, Egipto contra los pueblos del mar' in *Desperta Ferro, 6*

Gardiner, R., ed, *Conway's History of the Ship: The Age of the Galley* (London, 1995)

Gorelik, M., *Weapons of the Ancient East, IV Millennium BC–IV Century BC* (St Petersburg, 2003 - Russian language)

Grandet, P., *Le Papyrus Harris I (BM 9999)*, 2 vols (Bibliotheque d'etude, Cairo, IFAO, 1994)

Green, J., 'Forces of Transformation in Death: The Cemetery at Tell es-Sa'idiyeh, Jordan', in Bachhuber & Roberts, *Forces of Transformation: The End of the Bronze Age in the Mediterranean* - proceedings of international symposium, St John's College, University of Oxford, 25–26 March 2006 (*Themes from the Ancient Near East*, BANEA Publication 1, Oxford, 2009)

Green, J., 'Creating Prestige in the Jordan Valley: A Reconstruction of Ritual and Social Dynamics from the Late Bronze–Early Iron Age Cemetery at Tell es-Sa'idiyeh', in *Near Eastern Archaeology in the Past, Present and Future, Vol 1* - proceedings of 6th International Congress of Archaeology of Ancient Near East, 5–10 May 2009, 'Sapienza', Università di Roma (Matthiae, P., Pinnock, F., Nigro, L. & Marchetti, N., eds; Wiesbaden, 2009)

Guidotti, M.C. & Pecchioli Daddi, F., *La battaglia di Kadesh* (Firenze, 2002)

Gurney, O.R., 'The Annals of Hattusilis III', in *AnSt 47*(1997)

Hall, H.R., *Keftiu and the Peoples of the Sea* (Athens, 1902)

Hoelscher, U., *The Architectural Survey of the Great Temple and Palace of Medinet Habu, Season 1927–28, OIP 5* (Chicago University Press, 1929)

Houston, M., *Ancient Egyptian, Mesopotamian and Persian Costume* (New York, 2002)

Kanta, A., *The Late Minoan III Period in Crete: A Survey of Sites, Pottery and their Distribution* (Göteborg, 1980)

Karagheorghis, V., 'Cyprus in the 11th Century BC' -:proceedings of international symposium, Archaeological Research Unit, University of Cyprus, & Anastasios G. Leventis Foundation, Nicosia, 30–31 October 1993 (Nicosia, 1994)

Karagheorghis, V., *Excavations at Maa-Palaeokastro 1979–1986* (Nicosia; Dept of Antiquities, Cyprus, 1988)

Karageorghis, V., *Early Cyprus, Crossroads of the Mediterranean* (Los Angeles, 2002)

Killebrew, A. & Lehmann, G., *The Philistines and other 'Sea Peoples' in Text and Archaeology* (Atlanta, 2013)

Lilliu, G., *Sculture della Sardegna Nuragica* (Cagliari, 1966, 2008)

Murray, S.A., Smith, A.H. & Walters, H.B., *Excavations in Cyprus* (London, 1900)

Nelson, H.H., *The Epigraphic Survey of the Great Temple of Medinet Habu, Seasons 24–25 and 27–28, 1924–28* (Chicago University Press, 1929)

Nibbi, A., *The Sea Peoples and Egypt* (Park Ridge, 1975)

Oren, E.D., *The Sea Peoples and Their World: A Reassessment* (Philadelphia, 2000)

Rassu, M., *Shardana e Filistei in Italia* (Cagliari, 2003)

Robbins, M., *Collapse of the Bronze Age: The Story of Greece, Troy, Egypt, and the Peoples of the Sea* (Lincoln, 2000)

Rosellini, I., *I monumenti dell'Egitto e della Nubia, tomo primo, monumenti storici* (Pisa, 1932) Sandars, N.K., *The Sea Peoples* (London, 1978)

Schaeffer, C.F.A., *Les fouilles de Ras Ahamra-Ugarit, Syria 18* (1973)

Schofield, L. & Parkinson, R.B., 'Of Helmets and Heretics: A Possible Egyptian Representation of Mycenaean Warriors on a Papyrus from el-Amarna', in *BSA 89* (1994)

Serino, F., *L'antico Egitto di Ippolito Rosellini* (Seriate, 2003)

Stillman, N. & Tallis, N., *Armies of the Ancient Near East 3000BC–539BC* (Worthing, 1984)

Yadin, Y., *The Art of Warfare in Biblical Lands* (London, 1963)

Yalouris, N., 'Mykenische Bronzeschutzwaffen', in *AM 75* (1960)

Yasur-Landau, A., *The Philistines and Aegean Migration at the End of the Late Bronze Age* (Cambridge, 2010)

INDEX

DISCARD

Note: Page references in **bold** refer to photographs and captions. References in brackets refer to plate captions.